My Life and Times

1890 - 1919

Major Peter Cashin

Major and Mrs. Peter Cashin

My Life and Times

1890 -1919

MAJOR PETER CASHIN

Edited by R.E. Buehler

Breakwater Books Limited

Published by
Breakwater Books Limited
P.O. Box 52, Site C
Portugal Cove, Newfoundland A0A 3K0

Printed in Canada by
Robinson-Blackmore Printing
Publishing Co. Ltd.
18 O'Leary Avenue, St. John's, Newfoundland

Canadian Cataloguing in Publication Data

Cashin, Peter, 1890—
    Major Peter Cashin: my life and times

    Contents: v.1. 1890-1919
    ISBN 0-919948-24-3 (v. 1) pa.
    ISBN 0-919948-25-1 (v. 1) bd.

1. Cashin, Peter, 1890 — 2. Newfoundland — Politics and government — 20th century. * I. Buehler, Richard E., 1934—

FC2175.1.C38A3 1976   971.8'04'0924   C76-015033-8
F1123.C38

EDITOR'S NOTES

The practice among compilers and editors of affixing their names to other men's works has always seemed to me presumptuous. I now find myself in the position of affixing my name to another man's work. Be it said in my favour, however, that I chose one hell of a man with whom to associate my name.

Until recently I knew Peter Cashin only as a fiery patriot who, through his efforts to prevent Newfoundland's confederation with Canada, became a political legend in Newfoundland. Just now, when Major Cashin's old adversary, former Premier J.R. Smallwood, is beginning to doubt the wisdom of his efforts toward Confederation, have I come to know the Major personally. This book, a memorable trip with him through his old district of Ferryland, which gave me a chance to meet many of his former constituents, and countless cups of coffee shared with the Major and his very gracious wife in the comfort of their home have acquainted me with the warm, vibrant human being who is so much more than the legend. They have also done much to increase my understanding of and appreciation for Newfoundland.

Presumptuous I may be, but I am also grateful.

Dick Buehler
St. John's
Nov. 1976

CONTENTS

Introduction

Since retiring from active participation in public life in Newfoundland and after accepting the post of Director of Civil Defence for the province, I have been approached by numerous people to write my observations or memoirs on matters of public importance, which have taken place in this ancient island during the past half century. I have given this matter my most serious consideration and have come to the decision to prepare these personal and public observations, covering my own career, both private and public, particularly after the visit of the Honourable Patrick J. Little, who came to this island from Ireland at the invitation of the Smallwood government for the purpose of taking part in celebrations marking the first hundred years of Responsible Government in Newfoundland. Mr. Little received this invitation because he was the son of the first Prime Minister of Newfoundland when full Responsible Government was granted by the British government in 1855. Details of this particular matter are outlined in these memoirs.

I have been a politician, not a writer, for upwards of thirty years, and am taking this, my first opportunity of putting into book form my own personal experiences and memories dating back not alone to my own association in public life in this my native land, but also many particulars of interest on personal and public matters which have transpired since the turn of the present century.

For the uninitiated I would like to say something about Newfoundland and its early history. Newfoundland, exclusive of its dependency of Labrador, is an island of some forty-two thousand square miles. It is separated from the mainland of Canada at one point by approximately ninety miles and at the narrowest point by twenty-one miles. It has some six thousand miles of coastline, inundated with bays and coves, with many hundreds of which I am personally familiar. Its population is upwards of four hundred thousand souls. Indeed I love every rock, pond, harbour, lake, beach and patch of land which go to make up its rugged soil. This will all serve to make the reader more clearly understand something of the reasons why I fought so persistently and vainly in the past to preserve our original status — fought to prevent our becoming a poor relation of the Canadian nation. That of course is not my only purpose in writing these memoirs; but as I said before, this narrative will outline my own personal career and life. It outlines my "ups and downs" right up to the present day. The materials contained herein are factual and are indisputable. They are facts which reveal my own personal shortcomings, misdeeds and public actions. There is nothing withheld. Names of public men of the past and present are being mentioned as well as the part they played in the building up of this island; and particular reference is being made to those individuals who betrayed and sacrificed the best interests of Newfoundland for personal gain and prominence. The methods used by people in high places in both public and private life to sell out our country, just as we were about to enter a period of unprecedented prosperity, have been given in detail and documents have been used to prove these assertions. The parts played by the British and Canadian governments as well as the British-controlled Newfoundland Commission of Government have been told in full and proof has been given to show the unscrupulousness displayed in this great betrayal.

In preparing these volumes I have had to go back even to the days before my late father, Sir Michael Cashin, became a prominent figure in public life. I have had to recall the names of citizens long since gone. But, all in all, I think it will make interesting reading. I wish to dedicate these memoirs to the fine men and women of the historic district of Ferryland, who, for thirty years, continuously elected my father to the legislature as their representative and following this did me the great privilege of electing me to parliament on four different occasions.

Peter Cashin
St. John's
1955

Chapter I

My Early Childhood

I was born in Cape Broyle, Newfoundland, on March the 6th, 1890. My father was Michael P. Cashin, of Cape Broyle, and my mother, Gertrude C. Mullowney, of Witless Bay. Grandfather Richard Cashin was a fisherman planter in his settlement and Grandfather Pierre Mullowney was also a fisherman planter, as well as being one of the most successful sealing skippers of his time, having commanded sealing vessels at the seal fishery years before the advent of the steam sealing fleet.

Looking back, it is most difficult to give a full and accurate account of my early background and the background of my very ambitious parents. There are certain things with which I am well acquainted. My father, Michael P. Cashin, received the ordinary out-port education at Cape Broyle from the local teacher, at that time Mr. Cornelius Hartery, as well as Miss Grace, an old Irish lady who, for a short time, lived with my Grandfather Cashin. I well remember these two grand old people. Miss Grace later taught school in Brigus South and spent many of her holidays at our home in Cape Broyle. She was a charming, intellectual old lady. Mr. Hartery was the first teacher of my brother, Larry.

During the summer months my father, Michael Cashin, was one of the trap crew or cod seine crew with his father. Then, just before he reached his twentieth birthday, he was sent to St. Bonaventure's College for six months, and when he left there, his education now being finished, he was equipped to face the world with what is the equivalent today of ninth grade. He then entered the ships brokerage office, in St. John's, of the well-known firm of Michael Thorburn.

In the meantime John Cashin, Michael's elder brother, was conducting business at Cape Broyle. Michael, who had ambitions to get into business for himself, had a fair idea of the financial standing of his brother's business. He knew, for instance, that John owed several thousand dollars to the well-known firm of Bowring Brothers, Ltd. Therefore, when John died in 1886, Michael walked into Bowring's office, then under the management of Mr., later Sir Edgar, Bowring. He told Mr. Bowring that he would like to take over his brother's business and that, if his firm would give him the necessary financial backing in the form of credit, he would undertake to pay off his brother's debt to the Bowring firm. M.P. Cashin, as he was familiarly known, was then about twenty-two years old.

Bowring was fascinated by this most unusual proposition and accepted my father's proposal. Two banking vessels were acquired with the financial assistance of Bowring Bros., and whilst these vessels prosecuted the bank fishery for just a few short years before being lost at sea, their operation and management proved of wonderful help in the future expansion of this small outport fishing business.

My father, in addition to being strong of character, was physically powerful. He permitted nothing to stand in his way or impede his progress on the road to success. He tackled all kinds of obstacles and was successful in overcoming most of them. Let me give one example, not only of the determination of this man named M.P. Cashin, but also of his fighting capabilities. In those days there was no such thing as drawing lots for trap berths. In order to get what was considered the best trapping berth the crews competed with each other. In this particular instance my father was rowing the bow oar of his father's trap skiff. They had arrived at a place called Church Cove in Cape Broyle Bay about the same time as another crew under the leadership of a veteran trapman called Richard Walsh. A dispute arose and hot words were exchanged. It appears that one of Skipper Dick Walsh's crew, named John Lahey, a few years older than my father, insulted my grandfather. Mike Cashin immediately took up the cudgel for his father. He challenged Lahey to meet him in the old school-house meadow that same evening. In the fight which resulted, Cashin beat Lahey, then one of the strongest men in the harbour. This story was told me by old fishermen, long passed away, who witnessed the fight. In the small outport communities physical qualifications were essential to success both in business and politics.

Two years or less after taking over the Cape Broyle business, M.P. Cashin married Gertrude C. Mullowney, of Witless Bay. Father was then twenty-four years old and Mother was twenty-five. Gertrude Mullowney was a most ambitious and aggressive woman. She had the advantage of a much better education than my father. She began her education at the Presentation Convent, in Witless Bay, and completed it at St. Pierre. It is interesting to note that during her early school days, she and many other of the Mullowney girls were expelled from the convent school, because their fathers would not submit to be dictated to by the clergy as to which way they should vote politically. For asserting their independent spirit, the Mullowneys were christened the "Mad Dogs." Despite this, however, these fine women, none of whom are here today, remained loyal to their church, and in later years, when they had matured and become heads of families themselves, they contributed magnificently in the building up of schools and churches in Bay Bulls, Witless Bay and Cape Broyle.

The wedding, in the autumn of 1888, of Michael P. Cashin and Gertrude Mullowney was more than the matrimonial union of two young people. It was also a union of ambition and progress for the future. This marriage was a pooling of progressive spirits and proud traditions for the purpose of achieving personal advancement and material gain. It can truly be said that without the help of Gertrude Mullowney, M.P. Cashin would not have gone as far in the world as he did. We were told in our early years that all the money my father had when he married Gertrude Mullowney was forty dollars in cash and some thousands of dollars in debt, which he had obligated himself to pay on the demise of his brother, John Cashin. Never mind, work was a pleasure to both these great personalities. They worked hard themselves and expected others to do likewise.

When father and mother were first married they had no home of their own. They lived in my Grandfather Cashin's house for a few years. And so it came to pass that nine months after I was born, in March, 1890, I was taken to live with my Grandmother Mullowney in Witless Bay, where I was reared. I grew to look upon this charming, kindly and lovable old lady as my real mother. My mother's sister, Essie Mullowney, cared for me also, and nursed me as though I were her own child. I knew nothing of Cape Broyle and all its hustle and bustle. My brother Larry was born in Witless Bay in November, 1891. He was taken back to live in Cape Broyle, where my father had now built a small home.

In 1893, when I was but three years old, my father entered public life in Newfoundland. Naturally, I do not remember the actual election. Father was nominated as an independent candidate for his native district of Ferryland. His opponents were Daniel Joseph Greene and George Shea. These two men had already proved themselves political giants of that time. They looked with contempt upon any effort of this then insignificant man, Cashin, to break in on their prestige. In addition, they were strongly supported by the leaders of both church and state. However, when the votes were counted, following polling day, this man found himself at the head of the poll, having beaten both Greene and Shea by substantial majorities. M.P. Cashin was then twenty-nine years old. He had gained the confidence of the people because he was one of the people himself.

Michael P. Cashin arrived in Cape Broyle late in the night the day before nomination day. He had driven over the road from St. John's by horse and wagon, had announced his intentions at each settlement on the way, had friends canvassing for him the following day, just ten days before polling day. On arrival at Cape Broyle he found that Mother had long since gone to bed. He knocked at the door and Mother put her head out of her bedroom window to see who was there. Mike Cashin called to her to "open the door for the future member from Ferryland." Although he had never taken a drink of alcoholic beverage in all his life, this announcement led my mother to ask if he was drunk. The following day he was in Ferryland, the capital of the district, and had three men to propose, second and witness his nomination. (Two of these same old gentlemen did just that for me, thirty years later.) On the day of the counting of the ballots in Ferryland he met D. J. Greene, one of his opponents, on the road to St. John's. They talked about the campaign and Mr. Greene admitted he was defeated. My father replied that the two who would be elected would be Cashin and Greene, and his prediction came true. This left Mr. Shea the defeated candidate. On the opening of the House of Assembly in 1894 my father supported the Whiteway government as a back-bencher, sitting next to the late Judge W.H. Horwood, who, at that time, was also a member of the Whiteway party. Cashin was now thirty years old.

In between these periods my father had succeeded in doing a fair business, and as I said before, had now built his own home in Cape Broyle. My late brother, Richard, was born there in the year 1894 — the year of the "bank crash." My sister, Mary Fox, was born in Cape Broyle in January 1896. Well do I remember the occasion. As a youngster almost six years old, I listened to my Grandmother Mullowney and her sister, Aunt Frances Mullowney, discuss the forthcoming birth. In those days there was no such thing as women folk going to hospital for delivery. This applied particularly to the outports. The work was all performed by some of the finest women Newfoundland has ever produced. I remember my Grandmother Mullowney telling her sister that Gertie (my mother) was soon to give birth to another child and that Mrs. Getherall of Bay Bulls was going up with Mike (my father) for the occasion. I remember old Aunt Frances making some comments in this respect and as a child I was curious and had my ears cocked. Then my dear old grandmother, whom I affectionately called Moody, said to Aunt Frances to be careful of what she was saying, as "the child" was listening. I was the child in question and always sat in the old chair in the window of the dining room-parlour. I well remember my beloved old Moody saying, "Be careful, Frances, 'little pitchers have long ears'." That was evidently an old saying in those days to be careful what you were saying before children.

I remember the Newfoundland general election of 1897, when my father ran in Ferryland district for the second time. Strings were being pulled now to keep him from contesting the district. In other words, efforts were being made to "buy him off." He was approached in his own house at Cape Broyle by two of the most outstanding merchants of the day to stay out of the contest. These two St. John's merchants had a man they wanted to be elected. They promised my father that if he would do this, they would see that he was made magistrate of St. Mary's, which paid a salary at that time of not more than six hundred dollars yearly. It is not necessary to say that father turned this offer down. It was really an insult to his integrity and ability. He contested the election, having as his colleague, the late Martin W. Furlong, a nephew of my Grandmother Mullowney, and, in my opinion, the cleverest legal mind Newfoundland has produced, even to the present day. His record in the courts can show that. Furlong was defeated. My father and George Shea were elected. Father and Furlong ran under the banner of Sir William Whiteway, who himself was defeated in Trinity Bay, a constituency where he had been elected for years. The story goes that this political defeat broke Sir William Whiteway's heart. Sir James Winter became Prime Minister and formed what was generally termed a Tory Government. In those days the Tories carried the brand or stigma of being "the Merchants' Government."

The following year, 1898, was the year of the Reid deal or railway deal. There was a reshuffle of government and many of the Liberals voted for what was regarded by others as the notorious 1898 contract. This contract was made with Sir R. G. Reid to build a narrow gauge railway across the island of Newfoundland. The Reids, in addition to being paid to build, equip and operate the railway, were granted huge timber, mineral and water-power concessions. At one time it was stated that the Reids owned Newfoundland. Much difference of opinion as to whether or not the railway was beneficial to the country existed, but we cannot deny that the opening up of the interior of the island by the building of this narrow gauge railway was primarily responsible in later years for the development of the pulp and paper industry at Grand Falls and later at Corner Brook. Incidentally, during the passage

6

of this particular legislation in 1898, A.B. Morine, a Canadian by birth and a strong advocate of con- federation with Canada, occupied a prominent position in the Government. It transpired that Morine was also the legal adviser to the Reids and, because of this fact, was dismissed from office by the then Governor, H. H. Murray.

There are a few incidents which occurred during the 1897 election in Ferryland district which should be of interest, as well as being amusing, the details of which I learned from my father in later years. It appears that the settlement of Bay Bulls was split up considerably. Furlong felt that if Sir Edward Morris would come and address the people in an open-air meeting, it would be a great help to both himself and my father on polling day. Father did not agree with his colleague in this matter. Bay Bulls was one of the most independent com- munities in all Newfoundland. At that time the Grand Bank fishery was being prosecuted with vigor in that place and I am told that, at one time, there were twenty-seven banking vessels, commanded by twenty- seven Williamses of Bay Bulls, fishing on the Grand Banks. Father told Furlong, whose mother was a Williams from Bay Bulls, that if Morris came to ad- dress such a meeting he would not be there. Father felt that any intrusion by an outside person in the local election would be strongly resented by the people, and he was convinced that Morris would be driven out of Bay Bulls. Furlong had his way and the meeting was arranged for the night before polling day. My father stayed in Tors Cove that particular night. People from nearby settlements, hearing of the great Morris coming to Bay Bulls, drove by horse and even walked to witness this great meeting. The meeting was held in the open air on the gallery of Uncle Henry Williams' house. When Sir Edward rose to address the gathering he was greeted with boos, and was eventually sodded. The meeting was broken up and Furlong lost considerable votes which otherwise he might have received.

There was present at that meeting one Pierre Ronayne, of Tors Cove. Ronayne immediately realized the political effect such news would have if telegraphed to the southern end of the district. The telegraph offices were now closed and would not be open before morning. Ronayne drove at breakneck speed back to Tors Cove, arriving there at two or three o'clock in the morning. He knocked at the bedroom window of the house where my father was staying, Mrs. O'Driscoll's, on Tors Cove hill. Ronayne called aloud: "Wake up, Mike, wake up."; Father awoke, opened the room window and said: "What's wrong, Pierre?" Ronayne's reply was: "They have sodded Morris in Bay Bulls tonight. Will I cut the telegraph wires?" He did not want that bad news to reach the southern end of the district in the morning. "How are you going to cut the wires, Pierre?" asked my father. Pierre replied that he would climb up on a telegraph pole and cut them with two rocks. I need not tell you that this bad political news did not reach the southern end of the district until after all the voters had voted.

I cannot close this part of my narrative without making special mention of this grand old man, Pierre Ronayne. He was a very small man, not weighing more than eighty or eighty-five pounds. In an election campaign, or for that matter, any other controversy, Pierre Ronayne cared for nothing or nobody. He had no fear. He had a nerve of steel and his adversaries were generally men of great physical strength. The bigger and stronger they were, the more persistent Pierre was in his opinions. He would fight the biggest and the strongest of them on sight or at the drop of a hat. I have no hesitation in saying that there are no Newfoundlanders of his calibre left today. He lived to the ripe old age of ninety-five and I was honoured to have him act as my chairman in Tors Cove on two occasions, once in the election of 1923 and the second and last time in 1924. Well do I remember one morning during the campaign of 1924, when this old gentleman came to me outside Mrs. O'Driscoll's house. Calling me to one side, he said to me, "Peter, would five dollars be of any help to you?" Pierre Ronayne was always loyal to Cashin. With him, Cashin could do no wrong.

This man, Pierre Ronayne, took an active part in politics years before my father ever dreamed of entering public life. He took his politics seriously. He took an active part in the political campaign in which the late Judge L. G. Conroy stood as candidate for Ferryland. Ronayne was opposed to Mr. Conroy. He had a lot of personal followers in Tors Cove. He was one of the kings of Tors Cove, if not the real king. The clergy at that time were strongly supporting Mr. Conroy. Pierre Ronayne had made up his mind that Conroy would not hold a meeting in Tors Cove. He ascertained that the clergy were coming with Mr. Conroy to hold this particular meeting. He gathered his followers together, collected a few tubs of rotten squid (commonly called soldiers) and waited at the foot of Tors Cove hill for the arrival of the clergy and Conroy. Finally, two horses and square-body wagons hove in sight. Pierre Ronayne, then a very young man, lined up his followers to stop the passage of Conroy. The late Dean Roche walked towards Ronayne and ordered him to go back. Ronayne's reply was, "I will when me job is done. Conroy won't spake in Tors Cove tonight." Father Roche, then a very young priest, ordered the two carriages to come forward. Ronayne, undaunted, carried out his threat, and his followers, under his direction, threw the rotten squid at Conroy and they were forced to return. Ronayne had won his point for the time being. Many years later Ronayne, who owned and operated a Western boat named the *Mary Ellen*, was caught smuggling from the French island of St. Pierre. He was brought before the magistrate's court, which was presided over by Judge Conroy. Looking down over his glasses at Ronayne in that true Irish fashion, Judge Conroy is said to have made the remark, "Ronayne, I have got you at last," and condemned him to prison for a term of thirty days without the option of a fine.

Well, I have given a brief summary of political events from 1893-1897, when the Winter-Morine Government was returned to office and Sir William Whiteway and his Liberal Party were defeated. The construction of the cross country railway had begun. I was now seven years old. I had not yet gone to the local school in Witless Bay, but had learned my ABC and primer from my beloved Aunt Essie Mullowney, and was still living with my grandmother. In the autumn of 1897 I began going to the local boys' school, then under the able supervision of the late Mr. Joseph Long. Mr. Long stayed as teacher until the summer of 1898, when he obtained a government appointment as customs officer at Burin and later was transferred to a similar position at Marystown. He was occupying this position when I became Minister of Finance and Customs in the autumn of 1928, and on my appointment as Minister of the Crown, telegraphed me to the effect that he was proud of his old pupils in Witless Bay. The Presentation Nuns took over the educational work of both boys and girls at Witless Bay in the autumn of 1898. There I was taught by several of these fine, noble women, all of whom have since passed to their eternal reward. I was chosen as an altar boy and served mass for three years for the late Dean Roche and the late Reverend Father Michael O'Driscoll.

During these two or three years I was under the strictest of home discipline. My loving old Grandmother Mullowney would not permit me outside the gate to play with the other boys, and I was not permitted to go to school by myself for a couple of years. My guardian in that respect was selected by Granny, and each morning I had to wait for him to come and take me to school. He was the late Tommy Cotton of Witless Bay, who developed into one of nature's gentlemen.

To give you an idea of the discipline in this ideal Newfoundland home, let me say there were only certain places I was permitted to visit and play. In this respect I must mention my old friend, Ethel Mullowney, a cousin, who lived with Aunt Frances Mullowney, her grandmother. I was always permitted to go to old Mrs. Kate Mullowney's on the top of the hill. Ma, as I affectionately called her, was another wonderful old character. She was a widow, her husband, Patrick Mullowney, having been drowned on the Grand Banks on September 1st, 1890. Her daughter, Mary Jane, was my nurse during my first few years at Witless Bay. I have often heard Mary Jane relate how, on one particular day, I strayed away from her guidance and they all thought I had fallen in the old well near the house. But I turned up later and received a sound disciplinary lecture from that darling old grandmother, whose face is fresh in my memory after all these years.

During my ten years living with my Grandmother Mullowney at Witless Bay, I visited Cape Broyle with Aunt Essie Mullowney on a couple of occasions. To be quite frank, I did not like Cape Broyle at the time. As I said at the outset, I had grown to look upon Witless Bay as my natural home and my grandmother and Aunt Essie as my mother and guardian respectively. I very rarely saw my father or mother for more than half an hour, and this was when they were driving over the road from Cape Broyle to St. John's or St. John's to Cape Broyle, when they would stop at Witless Bay for a short rest. On the couple of occasions we visited Cape Broyle, we generally went there for the purpose of attending what was then called a "fancy fair" in aid of the church. On one of these occasions I remember meeting my Grandfather Cashin, who gave me a two dollar gold piece for a present, which on return to Witless Bay, I immediately deposited in my little black bank at the head of the hall stairs. I did not like Cape Broyle or anything in it. I wanted to get back, and cried to get back to my own darling grandmother. She was strict with me, but she was more than kind and affectionate. She loved me and I loved her more than I can express in words.

Around Christmas of 1897, my uncle Louis Mullowney was married to another lovable lady in the person of Miss Bride Walsh of St. John's. I remember the wedding supper on their return from St. John's that winter evening, when I was taken from my bed in my little room to come out and see my new aunt. Then, in December, 1898, a daughter was born of that union, and I well remember Uncle Louis coming up to the convent school to bring me down to be this new child's godfather.

I always looked forward to visits from my grandmother's younger brother, Mr. Henry Williams, of Bay Bulls, or Uncle Henry, as we called him. He came over nearly every Sunday to see her. I remember this old gentleman's profanity. I remember my dear old grandmother saying to him on numerous occasions, "Henry, the child is listening." Again, I was the child.

There were also many visits every week from Granny's sister, Aunt Frances Mullowney. The two sisters had married brothers. As I look back now, and think of these two old sisters, I recall the visits vividly of Aunt Frances down over the hill to see my grandmother, who was an invalid afflicted by rheumatism and who could just barely walk around the house. I recall their sociability of conversation on local and public matters with interest. They talked for hours over a cup of tea. Each had her own snuff-box and they interchanged their different qualities of that commodity, which they enjoyed snuffing in their noses, all the time discussing various topics, something similar to a couple of individuals of today discussing matters over a drink of whiskey and soda. Aunt Frances was a little more on the outspoken side than my grandmother, and at times her remarks were not what one would call appropriate for the ears of a child. They sat in two old rocking chairs opposite each other and when Aunt Frances made any kind of an inappropriate remark, she was always reminded by that loving grandmother of mine to be careful, as the child was listening, or, "that little pitchers had long ears." These two sisters were widows. My grandfather, Captain Pierre Mullowney, had died in 1892 and I do not remember him. Aunt Frances' husband, Mr. Stephen Mullowney, or, I should say, Uncle Stephen, had been a vessel builder in his time. He had built a Newfoundland fishing banker of some sixty-five tons for his two sons, Martin and Valentine Mullowney. This vessel was lost on the Grand Banks in a gale on September 1st, 1890. This tragedy of the sea is said to have killed Uncle Stephen, as, after the loss of the vessel, he is said to have stated that he had built a coffin for his sons and others of the Mullowney family. A model of this banking vessel was on exhibition in the old Newfoundland Museum for years, but once the Commission Government took over the administration of the affairs of Newfoundland, they began the scattering of all such things of historic interest. The Commission of Government destroyed the old Newfoundland Museum as well as the library of the House of Assembly. This was done with the approval of the British Government and three subservient

Newfoundland commissioners, who thought more of their jobs than they did of their country and its traditions.

On May the 24th, 1899, my brother, Martin, was born at Cape Broyle. He later became a medical doctor and had a brilliant scholastic career. Although unfortunate in many respects, he was, in my opinion, possessed of the most intelligent mind of all the Cashin family. Certainly he had the advantage of a better education than any of the family. I will go so far as to state that Martin, if he had been spared, would have been one of the outstanding diagnosticians in North America. He was a writer and lecturer of repute. Like my sister Mary's birth in 1896, I remember Aunt Frances Mullowney and Granny Mullowney discussing the forthcoming event. But this time Dr. McKenzie, an old Scots doctor, was brought over the road from St. John's by my father for the delivery. Father and Mother were now progressing rapidly in business and conditions in a general way were becoming brighter as years passed.

Then came a period in business which I remember slightly, when many steamers and vessels were wrecked around Cape Race in Trepassey and St. Mary's Bays. My father, ably assisted by my mother, had now gained the confidence of the well-known firm of Bowring Brothers, Ltd., who at that time, were exclusive agents for Lloyds of London in Newfoundland. Bowrings gave him the opportunity to handle the cargoes of wrecked goods and to refloat, when possible, wrecked vessels or steamers. M.P. Cashin had now become a public figure, as well as an expert in the art of handling wrecks. His political opponents in later years christened him the "King of Wrecks." The fishermen along that part of the coast were adept in wrecking and, in many cases, in looting these tragedies of the sea. Cashin was the only man who could handle these fishermen and he did so with a stern hand. In those days these same fishermen looked forward annually, particularly in the spring and early summer, to a wreck or wrecks to provide part of their annual income. Working at wrecks during the early part of the present century may be regarded as part of the economic life of a goodly number of the fishermen in that particular territory.

Let me give you two examples of the manner in which M. P. Cashin handled some of these difficult jobs. In the first place he had to establish himself as a leader amongst these fishermen. On many occasions, to establish that leadership, he was forced to use his physical qualities. When physical methods were necessary to handle some of these difficult situations, M. P. Cashin walked right in and he certainly "handled them rough." He was capable of doing this, and the fishermen grew to admire him because he was.

On one occasion a steamer was stranded in the vicinity of Cappahayden. Mike Cashin was there on the old *Grand Lake* with Mr. Henry Bowring and others. Neither Bowring nor any of his associates had the know-how to handle such situations. Many passengers were aboard this particular vessel. The sea was rough and the ship's crew were trying to land the passengers on the beach in lifeboats. Their efforts were anything but successful. The lifeboats were being upset and many lives were being endangered. Mr. Bowring came to my father and said, "Michael, how can we land these passengers?" My father, waiting for this opportunity, replied that he was prepared to land the several hundred passengers on a contract. He then made a written contract with Bowring, Lloyd's agent. Immediately the contract was signed, he jumped into a dory with two other fishermen, rowed out around the many fishing boats and jacks anchored off shore, which had been fishing on Cape Ballard Bank. Each boat, or jack, carried two dories. Cashin hired all the dories, paying the fishermen handsomely for their work. Dories are the best of sea boats when handled by men who know how to manipulate them. The fishermen in that territory in those days were experts in handling these tiny craft. All the passengers were landed safely, and now M. P. Cashin was an independent man. He had made sufficient money on that particular day to pay off his brother's debt to Bowring's and have a goodly balance left for himself.

Then came the wreck of the *Scottish King* on November 30, 1898. This ship was loaded with a most valuable cargo which was salvaged on a percentage basis, the vessel being later refloated, and towed to St. John's for temporary repairs on our local dry dock. Cashin was now in the "big money" for those days. Wrecks were numerous and M.P. Cashin was always to be found on the job. I cannot refrain from telling a couple of stories regarding the salvaging of the cargo of the *Scottish King*. My father had taken charge of this job on a contract. However, certain brokers or representatives of St. John's commercial houses had come to the wreck to attempt to take over the difficult work. In one case a representative of one of the out-standing firms still doing a large business on Water Street attempted to bully M. P. Cashin. He drew a revolver and threatened to shoot him. Even this did not in any way frighten Cashin. He sailed right in, beat up his would-be assailant, who then recognized that discretion was the better part of valour and retired from the scene of the wreck. This particular story was told me by the late Mr. Harry Saunders, who at that time was a telegraph operator with the old Anglo-American Telegraph Company, and who had been sent to the scene of the wreck to establish direct contact with St. John's.

As I said in the early part of this chapter, M.P. Cashin never took a drink of alcoholic beverage in all of his life. He said after the wreck of the *Scottish King* to an old friend that he was only tempted once to take a drink of alcohol. It appears that during the many days or weeks it took to salvage the cargo of the *Scottish King*, one evening the wind started to blow heavy, eventually reaching gale force. The sea became rough and it looked as if the wrecked vessel must be broken up. All the fishermen working at the discharge of this most valuable general cargo left the vessel. Only three people remained. They were the mate, another friend and partner of my father in the venture, Mr. Tasker Cook, who came from St. John's, and my father. They decided to stay aboard and take a chance. The mate went down in the hold of the wrecked ship and brought up a case of champagne and a case of whiskey. There was plenty of such cargo aboard. The mate and father's associate in the venture proceeded to get intoxicated and eventually fell asleep. During all this time M. P. Cashin was awake. He realized the danger they were exposed to. He did not know what minute the ship would be broken in pieces by the raging sea and they be drowned. The other two, now intoxicated, knew nothing of the danger to their lives and the mixture of champagne and whiskey had its effect in making them forget any of their worries. My father was looking at them both apparently sleeping peacefully. He said afterwards that it was the only time he was tempted to take that drink. However, he stuck it out and before morning the wind veered, the seas calmed down, the fishermen came aboard and when the other two woke from their drunken stupor, Cashin was busy supervising the discharge of the wrecked cargo. Does not this action alone show the strong will-power and fearless determination of this ambitious man?

I cannot refrain from telling just one more amusing story regarding the handling of these wrecks. A ship became stranded around Cappahayden, which had now been christened the "graveyard of the Atlantic." Bowring's asked M. P. Cashin to go there and handle the situation. Cashin was in St. John's at the time, a distance of sixty-five miles from the scene of the disaster. Bowring's telegraphed the captain that a man called Cashin was on his way to take charge of the salvaging, etc. It was a long tedious drive by horse and buggy over the road. The fishermen around this territory had gotten aboard the ship and begun their work of destruction and looting. They generally went after the copper and brass on the engines if they could not get at the cargo. They never paid any attention to the master of the ship. M.P. Cashin eventually arrived on the scene. He was greeted on the beach by one Mr. Edward ("Neddy") O'Leary, of Renews, who was wreck commissioner. This old gentleman was another great character of his time. Immediately, they proceeded to board the ship by dory. Old man O'Leary was sitting in the stern of the dory, whilst my father was standing in the middle between the two fishermen who were rowing the boat. Finally, they reached the side of the stranded vessel. A rope ladder was hanging over the side. Father proceeded to climb aboard the ship. The captain was on the bridge, all flustered and worried. The fishermen had taken charge and were cleaning out the wrecked ship. The captain looked over the side and shouted, "Is that you, Cashman?" Father replied, "Yes." The captain cried aloud to this man, "Cashman," to "come aboard, they are robbing me, they are robbing me!" The old man, O'Leary, who wore a long venerable white beard, and was renowned for his Irish wit and quaint remarks, looked up towards the distressed captain on the bridge and shouted back, "Well, the king of the robbers is going up to you now."

During the early part of the present century, wrecks of steamers and vessels were very prevalent along that part of the coast around Cape Race. It is a well known fact that all steamers and vessels coming from Europe and heading westward towards Canada and the United States, had to make Cape Race in order to take their course for the North American continent. There was no such thing as wireless telegraphy or direction finding apparatus. In the early spring and summer the prevailing fogs and tides frequently dragged ships off their course and in many cases they were stranded and became wrecked. It seems that during the first ten years of the present century, wrecks of ships along that part of the coast were eagerly looked forward to, as I have already stated, as a part of the economic life of St. Mary's and Trepassey Bays, as well as between Cape Race and Fermeuse. It was not considered a crime to steal from a wrecked vessel. Nevertheless, it was generally conceded that M. P. Cashin always had full charge of the salvaging of these ships and their cargoes. A lot of his time was spent away from Cape Broyle, whilst the Cashin stores were always filled with wrecked goods of some kind or another.

Whilst M. P. Cashin was absent from his business at Cape Broyle, he had a wonderful, capable partner in the person of my mother, Gertrude Mullowney Cashin. She knew the fish business from beginning to end, or rather, should I say she was most proficient in the operation of fishing traps, the baiting and supplying of American and Nova Scotia vessels, the supplying of ice and the purchase of cod oil from these various fishing bankers, as well as the general management of an outport fishing business. I repeat what I have said earlier in this chapter, that without her assistance, without her energy and know-how, M. P. Cashin could not possibly have carried on the work he had set himself to perform. If Mike Cashin made one dollar, Gertie Cashin made half of it. As a matter of fact, I am of the opinion that my mother was capable of getting more work out of men than my father himself. She had that peculiar way of doing things that appealed to the working men around the premises.

In the month of September, 1900, I was taken away from my adopted home with my Grandmother Mullowney in Witless Bay and brought to St. Bonaventure's College, for what at the time was considered advanced education in all its moods and tenses. Well do I remember the month of August, 1900, when my father arrived at Witless Bay and told my dear old Grandmother Mullowney as well as my Aunt Essie Mullowney, that when St. Bonaventure's College opened in September, I was to be put there boarding to get that additional education. And well do I recollect the hustle and bustle as well as the excitement of the following two or three weeks, with my aunt getting a supply of new clothes ready, getting them marked with my name or initials and finally getting that little trunk packed. Oh, how well do I remember the first day that I left the arms of my dear old grandmother and my dear Aunt Essie, to be brought to that college by my father; and how in that first evening of my stay in St. Bon's I got into a fistic encounter with Lance Phippard, who later became my close friend and school companion.

I was first put in what would be termed the primary class with two teachers, one Brother Fennessy and the other Brother Norris. Brother Fennessy always remained one of my staunchest friends. Brother Norris did not remain long at the College after my arrival. He was transferred back to Ireland and in his place came Brother Daly. For the first few months of that autumn quarter, the college was under the supervision of Brother Lavelle, but he was transferred to South Africa and in his place came Brother Downey, whom we all feared. During that first quarter I was introduced to subjects such as geometry, algebra, French and shorthand; all of which were unfamiliar to me. Naturally, it took me some considerable time before I could get into the new routine.

We received our two weeks holidays at Christmas, 1900, and I spent that two weeks with my grandmother and Aunt Essie at Witless Bay. I did not want to go to my parents at Cape Broyle. However, I involved myself in what was then considered serious trouble. During my first few months at St. Bon's I had learned to play football, and felt that if I had a football to bring back with me to Witless Bay, I would show off what a wonderful fellow I was to the boys in that place. What did brave Peter do? I went down to Bowring's, where I knew my father had an account, a few days before I left with the mailman for Witless Bay, procured a football, and charged it to him. I remember the price to this very day. It was two dollars and fifty cents. To my utter surprise and terror a few days later, after I had returned to Witless Bay and was showing off my prowess to the young boys of that place in the manly sport of football, my father arrived on his way home to Cape Broyle. What did he do? He had received the bill for the football. He was infuriated with me. So, he took the football from me and brought it away with him to Cape Broyle. Had it not been for the intervention of my beloved grandmother, I know I would have received a sound thrashing at my father's hand.

During the autumn of 1900 a general election took place in Newfoundland. Again, my father contested the district of Ferryland on behalf of the Liberal Party under the leadership of Sir Robert Bond. Bond had now superseded Sir William Whiteway as leader of the Liberal Party. The Liberal Party went to the country pledged to revise some of the concessions granted to the Reids under the railway contract act of 1898. My father's colleague at this time was the late Honourable J.D. Ryan, a well-off Irishman, who had made considerable money on the sale of liquor, and who controlled various retail liquor stores throughout the city of St. John's. Cashin and Ryan were elected easily. Mr. Ryan had the strong support of all the clergy, and this, added to my father's personal popularity, made the campaign an easy one. This was the third time M. P.

Cashin was elected for his native district. He never looked upon any political campaign as easy. He always felt that the election was not won until the last ballot was counted. He always visited every home in the district and kept in personal contact with the people at all times. He never omitted answering the letters of his constituents, even though, on numerous occasions, he would have to reply in the negative to requests made by individuals. My own personal experience tells me that father was correct in this view. The prompt answering of letters from your constituents is of great political value. M. P. Cashin was strong on the matter of telling his constituents whether or not it was possible to do certain things they might request him to do. If he felt their request was justified he strained all efforts possible to accede to their request. On the other hand, if the request sounded unjustifiable, unnecessary or unreasonable, he never failed to tell them so. There was no such thing as beating about the bush by this man Cashin. It was either yes or no with him and that ended it. Such a policy paid off politically in the final analysis and because he was forthright on such matters, M. P. Cashin became the guide, philosopher and friend of the people of Ferryland district.

There are a few incidents which might be of interest to the public which took place during the election of 1900. At a public meeting in Ferryland proper, a certain group of political opponents tried to break up the Cashin-Ryan meeting in the Star Hall. A regular brawl ensued, and in the middle of this brawl was to be found Mike Cashin. He could stand what he considered the nonsense no longer, so he threw off his coat, jumped from the platform, beat up a couple of individuals who were the ring-leaders of the trouble and wound up by being defended by his former colleague of 1897, Martin W. Furlong, before a jury in the Supreme Court. Needless to say, the jury acquitted Cashin. Innocent (politically) J. D. Ryan was flabbergasted. He could not understand such tactics and in any case, was incapable of handling such a situation.

Then, just one more outstanding incident with respect to this 1900 general election. My mother, who was just as enthusiastic and aggressive politically as she was commercially, was serving Mr. Ryan his breakfast one morning shortly before polling day. This old gentleman, J. D. Ryan, felt that, because he had the special support of the clergy of the district, it was possible that he might head the poll in this election and beat my father. He asked my mother when she was serving him some ham and eggs, "Do you think I will beat Mike?" Mother, who was quick on the uptake, replied, "You will be damned lucky if you are elected."

The Bond Liberal Government was elected by an overwhelming majority, and immediately took the necessary legal steps to revise some of the concessions granted the Reids under the 1898 railway contract, particularly with respect to timber concessions and telegraph concessions. The matter finally ended before the Privy Council in London, resulting in the Newfoundland Government having to pay the Reids over one million dollars for the recovery of the telegraph system and a slight modification of some of the other concessions. Also, it was during or about this time that the Nova Scotia Steel & Coal Company and the Dominion Coal Company, which were two separate companies at that time, acquired from John and Jabez Butler, of Topsail the iron mines on Bell Island. The price they paid for this valuable property was less than one hundred thousand dollars. It was really a gift to these two particular companies, who were manufacturing steel and other products in their mills in Sydney, Nova Scotia. Development of these valuable resources began immediately, which resulted in the bringing into production of the largest iron ore property in the world. I will have more to say about these two companies in a later chapter of these memoirs.

For the next six years I was a boarding student at St. Bonaventure's College. Well do I remember when I returned there after my first Christmas holidays, just after New Year, 1901, how I cried like the child that I was to get back again to my dear old grandmother in Witless Bay. For the first few nights after these holidays I cried myself to sleep. I cannot forget that wonderful old Brother Prendergast (whom we all called the Boss) trying to console me and telling me that I would be alright. That phase of my life lasted only a few days until I got into the swing of things with the other boys and became quite happy, even though I might not have been too studious.

At that time there were only thirty boarders at the College and we slept in the old dormitory. We had our special mornings for baths and the water was very seldom warm. Our boy prefects during those six years were such outstanding men as the late Reverend Father Pippy, George Malcolm, later a professor of English in some Italian university in Rome, Italy, and John Penney, later a Rhodes scholar and professor of languages at Harvard University in the United States.

We boarders did not go home for the Easter holidays. They were too short and transportation facilities were not as easy as today, so we spent those few days holidays in the college. The boys were permitted to go out to town every afternoon, although some of us were restricted, as our parents had given the Brother Superior instructions not to permit us to go out to town except to certain places. Why, it was a wonderful event when some one in town invited you out to dinner, and it was still more pleasant when Mother came to St. John's, as she frequently did on business, and took me down to Wood's old candy store for a good meal. Then, probably on a Sunday, when Father would be in town, he might take me down to the Crosbie Hotel, the old Tremont Hotel, and later the Balmoral Hotel for a square meal.

During the summer holidays, which came around the first week in July, I was being gradually educated to be content to live in Cape Broyle with my parents. At first it was a very tough proposition. I did not like the place at that time, and always wanted to get back to Witless Bay to my affectionate old Grandmother Mullowney. My education in transferring myself, or might I say, having my affections for Witless Bay lured away towards Cape Broyle, was begun and continued by my accompanying my mother on her many trips over the road from Cape Broyle to St. John's and return, a distance of forty miles each way. Mother took me along as company for her during her night driving. She often made as many as four or five trips a week over that narrow, winding old road, on business. She generally stopped to see my grandmother at Witless Bay, took me along with her to St. John's, and it was not unusual for us to return to Cape Broyle the same night. It was a long, hard and tedious trip in the dark and sometimes rainy nights, but the bad weather never interfered with mother's business program. She always drove the horse herself and it was not until years later that I was permitted to drive. Mother could handle a horse with any man. She had no fear, even though our horses were always fast and sometimes in difficult parts of the road, were anything but co-operative. Father would be at home or at a wreck, and mother had to go to St. John's to do the business of buying goods of all kinds, seeing that the coasters were loaded quickly and on their way back to Cape Broyle without any delay.

The Cape Broyle business was now expanding at great speed. At that time, particularly during the months of June, July and August, it was not unusual to see forty American and Nova Scotia banking vessels anchored in Cape Broyle, taking bait, ice and other supplies. The Cashin enterprise was getting the greater portion of this profitable business. Blubber had to be landed, cod oil to be gauged, ice to be delivered and settlement of accounts adjusted, whilst in addition, two or three trap crews had to be managed on the same premises. Gertrude Cashin was capable of doing this work even better than her husband. Transportation facilities at that time were confined to one coastal boat every two weeks. There was no thought of a railway ever being built along the Southern Shore. All goods and supplies had to be carried in small freighters of not more than thirty tons each. Motor cars or trucks did not exist. Motor engines for boats were not even dreamed of, and everything depended for speed on a fair wind for the coaster, two pairs of oars for a dory and four eighteen foot spruce oars and a sculling oar for a trap skiff.

One particular incident which occurred during one of these many journeys over the Cape Broyle — St. John's road may be of interest. It happened one night in July of 1903. We arrived at Mrs. O'Driscoll's in Tors Cove on our way back to Cape Broyle. Mrs. O'Driscoll was a charming old lady as well as a great personal friend of the Cashin family. She kept the post office and telegraph office. We stopped off there to feed the horse and have a cup of tea. Immediately we entered the kitchen Mrs. O'Driscoll said to my mother, "Mrs. Cashin, an awful thing happened in Cape Broyle this evening." "What was that, Mrs. O'Driscoll?" "Oh," she said, "Captain Woollard, an American banking skipper, shot a man belonging to his crew, called Yetman." John Yetman, incidentally, came from St. Mary's. The greater number of the crew, including the captain, had been drinking heavily the night before. The anchor had been weighed, the sails set and the vessel, the *Helen F. Whitten*, was headed out through the harbour, bound for the Grand Banks. Yetman, who wanted to leave the vessel, came aft and told Captain Woollard that he was going ashore. There was a dory being towed astern of the vessel. Woollard told Yetman that if he dared to leave the ship he would be sorry. Yetman pulled up the dory, jumped aboard and immediately tried to cut the painter with his sheath knife. As he did this, Woollard fired four shots from his revolver into Yetman's body, killing him instantly. The mate, Joseph Walsh, who was apparently mixed up with the drunken row the night before, came aft, knocked Woollard down, took the wheel, brought the vessel up in the wind and turned her back into the harbour. Walsh came from Point Verde, Placentia Bay. The local police officer, Mr. Greene, boarded the vessel, arrested Woollard, whose given name was Francis, and brought him to jail in Ferryland.

On hearing this news from Mrs. O'Driscoll, we immediately set out for Cape Broyle. My mother did not spare the horse that night. We made the twelve mile journey in just a little over an hour. On arrival at Cape Broyle, father informed us of what had happened. He told us that he had telegraphed Martin Furlong to come immediately, that some ten American fishing skippers had subscribed one hundred dollars each to procure counsel to defend Woollard. Furlong arrived during the night with Matt. Kelly, that old reliable St. John's cabman. After having had some supper at our house, they went on to Ferryland to see Woollard. The following day the accused was brought over the road to

St. John's. I remember them stopping at our store at Cape Broyle, so that Woollard could sign the ship's bills. The police officer took the handcuffs off him for this purpose and he was permitted to shake hands with my mother.

Woollard was charged with murder, but Furlong succeeded in getting him off with manslaughter. Sir Edward Morris was attorney general at that time and it was his ambition to get a conviction and beat Furlong. Woollard did not serve anything like the sixteen year sentence, but was released a few years later, and I have been told, came down to Bay of Islands afterwards, in charge of a vessel buying frozen herring for the American market. My father was present in the Supreme Court when the trial took place. He told me later that Furlong's address to the jury was one of the greatest pieces of oratory he had ever heard. In fact, he had several of the jurors in tears. That particular case was instrumental in establishing Martin W. Furlong as the outstanding criminal lawyer of the time. His practice grew, his firm grew. He later became director of the Reid Newfoundland Company and their special legal adviser.

As I grew older, I was brought back to Cape Broyle for the summer holidays. These days were not really holidays for me. I was made work at fish, at hay and at all kinds of other labouring work around the premises. For instance, every Saturday evening it was customary with my father to have the main road leading through Cape Broyle, particularly opposite our own property, swept clean. Together with other men working around the place at fish, ice, etc., I was made join in this cleaning up process of the main road, which father insisted should be done for Sunday. He certainly was a demon for cleanliness. He wanted to see every house in Cape Broyle painted and limed. I was now gradually being weaned away from good old Witless Bay and missed the affection of my dear old grandmother. Even at that, I never forgot her kindness to me, and many times when I had petty troubles, and that was frequently, I went to her somehow or another for consolation and guidance. I did this because during the first ten years of my life I saw very little of my father or mother, except when they were passing through Witless Bay on their way to or from St. John's or Cape Broyle.

As I have already pointed out, I was not what one would term a studious individual. As I remember those good old St. Bon's days, I do not remember concentrating too much on my studies or lessons. I was one of those harum-scarum individuals, violated many of the school regulations and was administered the punishment I deserved on such occasions. I was associated in classes with such outstanding scholars as Jack McGrath, Jack Fox, Jack Higgins, D.A. Flynn, Tommy Lamb and others. I was just an ordinary school boy and felt myself lucky to pass my preliminary and intermediate grades. If there was such a thing as my concentrating on any particular subjects, these were shorthand, typewriting and arithmetic. I had the privilege of typewriting the recommendations by Reverend Brother Culhane for John Penney, who was a candidate for the Rhodes scholarship on two occasions. He won it the second time. I was proud of John Penney and looked upon him as an ideal scholar. He was not what I would call exceedingly brilliant, but he was a plodder and worker. He had determination and ambition. Penney was an ideal character in every respect.

One great privilege I had during my six years at St. Bonaventure's College was that of being chosen by Reverend Brother Fennessy as one of the two boys amongst the boarding students to serve mass for the late Archbishop Howley. The archbishop was most gentle and kind. I cannot remember how many times I had the nerve to ask His Grace to come into the college some time during the day and ask the brothers to give us a holiday. A few times he acceded to my request. I have always looked upon the late Archbishop Howley as our most patriotic and loyal Newfoundlander. There was no such thing with him as sectarianism or bigotry. He was fearless, and never hesitated to express his views on matters of general interest to the people of Newfoundland as a whole.

During these years as a boarding student at St. Bon's, I was frequently invited to the homes of Mrs. James McGrath, Mrs. Dr. Keegan and Captain Edward

English Sr., who at that time was harbour master. The Brother Superior had to have special permission from my parents to permit me to go to the homes of these hospitable people, all of whom were more than kind to me. Mrs. Keegan was a most interesting person and a real mother. She knew Newfoundland and Newfoundlanders as few other people did. She was a well-educated woman, had been at school with my mother at St. Pierre. She was undoubtedly a keen political observer on Newfoundland public matters and in many cases had given political advice on public affairs to members of parliament both in the Cabinet and on the backbenches.

Mrs. James McGrath was the mother of Dr. Jim McGrath, former Minister of Public Health. Her husband died in Halifax during the year 1902. Mrs. McGrath did not lay down after the passing of her husband. She went into business as proprietress of the old Balmoral Hotel, opposite the general post office. She became interested in other business matters and made a success of all of them. Dr. McGrath had been governor of H.M. Penitentiary for several years. He was a most astute politician and represented the district of Placentia and St. Mary's for several years. Mr. McGrath was a particular friend of my father. I always enjoyed my visits to the McGrath home, and before Mr. McGrath's death, his son, Jack, and myself used to play in the old penitentiary yard. Jack turned out to be one of the most brilliant scholars this island has ever produced. He was a candidate for the Rhodes scholarship, was turned down, went to Dalhousie University at Halifax. During his summer holidays from the university he went to New York and succeeded in getting jobs as secretary to individuals or organizations, jobs obtained through the good influence of his uncle, Captain John W. McGrath, who conducted a flourishing stevedore business in many of the Atlantic seaboard ports. Finally, Jack became private secretary to the late President Theodore Roosevelt, and, just as he was about to become one of the outstanding financiers in the United States, died at the early age of thirty-one in the year 1922. He had become identified with George Perkins, a financial magnate of outstanding qualities in New York and Boston. It may be of interest to note at this time that Jack McGrath, the year after his father's death in 1902, became a shorthand reporter in our local House of Assembly at the age of twelve years. I have been told by reporters many years his senior that McGrath was the ablest of them all.

In the autumn of 1904 another general election took place in Newfoundland, and again my father contested the district of Ferryland on behalf of the Liberal Party, again under the leadership of Sir Robert Bond. In 1895 the Bell Island mines had been brought into production by the Nova Scotia Steel and Coal Company and, from 1899, was operated by that company and the Dominion Coal Company. These two companies merged in 1921. Work in Conception Bay was plentiful. The cross country railway was in operation and contracts had been given the Reids for the building and operating of a much improved coastal boat system to service the island. In addition, the possibilities of the establishment of a pulp and paper mill at Grand Falls added further prestige to the Bond Party. My father's colleague for this election was the late W.J. Ellis, a prominent Newfoundland contractor, one of nature's gentlemen and a man of unblemished character. Both father and Mr. Ellis were elected with substantial majorities, and M. P. Cashin headed the poll for the fourth successive time. The Bond Government was elected by an overwhelming majority. Out of thirty-six House of Assembly members, the Liberal party had won thirty-two, leaving the opposition under the leadership of the late Alfred B. Morine with just four members.

During the year 1905, when the legislature convened, the Bond Government introduced legislation known as the ''Foreign Fishing Vessels Act,'' the provisions of which prohibited American fishing vessels which fished on the Newfoundland Grand Banks from taking bait and supplies on the Newfoundland coast. Representations had been made by the bank fishing interests of Newfoundland as well as, indirectly, by the Nova Scotia banking fleet, which, in effect, asked the government of the day to give protection to our own local bank fishermen as well as the Nova Scotia fleet. My father did not see eye to eye with Sir Robert Bond in this particular legislation, and as a result he crossed the floor of the legislature and established himself as an Independent member. His colleague, Mr. Ellis, remained with the Bond Government, and, although they were politically opposed to each other because of this particular legislation, they always remained the closest of personal friends. It can be truly said that the deviation of M. P. Cashin from the Bond Government ignited the spark which ultimately resulted in the defeat of the Liberal party in 1909 and the coming into power of "The People's Party," under the leadership of Sir Edward Morris.

During the session of the legislature in 1905 the Bond Liberal government introduced legislation which was responsible for the establishment of the pulp and paper mill at Grand Falls. The credit for the establishment of this now flourishing industry may be attributed to the energy and negotiating abilities of the late H. J. Crowe, a Canadian lumber man. Mr. Crowe had been successful in obtaining certain timber licences in the Exploits Valley territory and also had secured options on other timber properties which were leased to private individuals. Crowe was successful in selling the idea of the establishment of a paper mill in this area to the Harmsworth brothers, later Lords Northcliffe and Rothermere. These two Englishmen controlled a large chain of newspapers in the United Kingdom and their policy was to manufacture their own newsprint, so as not to be dependent on outside manufacturers for their large supply of this commodity. The mill at first did not have a capacity of much more than one hundred tons daily. Whilst I cannot refrain from criticizing the Northcliffe group for their efforts at blocking another similar industry in Newfoundland, nevertheless they are to be commended for their speculative endeavours.

At the beginning of this operation, these two newspaper geniuses took good care to see that the Grand Falls mill showed a loss on operation. A special company was incorporated under Newfoundland law to operate this mill. The company was named the Anglo-Newfoundland Development Company Ltd., and production of newsprint began in December of 1909. The shares of the company were listed on the London stock exchange, and its annual reports at first always showed a loss on operation, whilst their huge newspaper chain was showing increased profits. They were, in fact, selling the newsprint to themselves. Their idea was to block any effort by the Reid Newfoundland Company, which had considerable timber land in the Humber area, to promote another pulp and paper company. However, at the end of the first World War, the Northcliffe-Rothermere group were caught at their game. Profits or corporation taxes became so high in Great Britain that they decided they would show the legitimate profit on newsprint to their Newfoundland Company, as these same taxes were practically nothing in Newfoundland. Thus it became known to the financial world that Grand Falls (the A.N.D. Co.) had always been a paying proposition, and later, as I will relate in these memoirs, the Reids were able to interest financial concerns in Great Britain, as well as the British government, in the establishment and development at Corner Brook of what was the largest pulp and paper mill in the entire world.

Sir Robert Bond, the then leader of the Liberal party and prime minister of Newfoundland, was a highly cultured gentleman. He had been born in luxury. He had studied law for a few years but was never admitted to the Bar. He had a superiority complex. He was honest in his convictions, but was, undoubtedly, arrogant and an autocrat. He had been in public life for many years and had done considerable good work for Newfoundland. At one time he went so far as to pledge his private fortune as security for a loan on the credit of Newfoundland which the British government had absolutely refused to endorse. In fact, Bond was probably our only real statesman. He was not a politician in the strict sense of the word. He lived a secluded life on his estate at Whitbourne, which, according to the terms of his will, went, after his death, to the Newfoundland government for the purpose of establishing an experimental farm. Bond had been Colonial Secretary to the Whiteway government, and in that capacity, had made a treaty or agreement with the United States government, the provisions of which treaty would give favourable tariff concessions to Newfoundland for the marketing of her fishery products in the great United States of America. This particular agreement was known as the Bond-Blaine Treaty. However, the Canadian government, jealous of our possibilities of marketing our fish in America, used its influence with the British government to have this treaty set aside. The British ambassador in Washington at the time was instructed by the "powers that be" in Downing Street to request the American government not to ratify this particular treaty. Washington then succumbed to the pressure of London and Ottawa. Newfoundland, Britain's oldest colony, was betrayed by the British government. This action on the part of the American government undoubtedly created considerable prejudice and vindictiveness in Sir Robert Bond's mind, and he took full advantage of the first possible opportunity to retaliate and get even with our American friends.

On the other hand, my father represented a district where numerous American fishing vessels had the privilege of procuring bait and supplies in the various harbours along the Southern Shore of Newfoundland. It meant thousands of dollars annually to the fishermen of Ferryland district, particularly in places like Bay Bulls, Cape Broyle, Calvert and Aquaforte. Cashin felt that he would be betraying the interests of these people if he supported such legislation and consequently resigned from the Bond Liberal party. Nevertheless, at that time, some of his former associates had the view that he (Cashin) left the Bond party because he did not get a cabinet seat in that government. This view was particularly stressed by the late Honourable E. M. Jackman, at that time Minister of Finance and Customs in the Bond government. He stood up in the House of Assembly and accused my father on these grounds. Jackman went so far as to state that the late Archbishop M.F. Howley had told him (Jackman) that my father had asked His Grace the Archbishop to intercede on his behalf with Sir Robert Bond. This charge my father flatly and emphatically denied. A heated debate took place in the House on the matter. Unparliamentary language was not uncommon and the Speaker at that time, Honourable F.J. Morris, had his hands full keeping order. It appeared that certain parties had gone to the archbishop and requested the archbishop to use his influence with Sir Robert Bond in my father's interest. After Jackman had made that charge in the House of Assembly, my father immediately contacted Archbishop Howley, demanding from him without delay, a letter to the effect that he (Cashin) had never approached him (the archbishop) on such a matter. He received that letter the same day and had it published in the *Evening Telegram*. This communication from the archbishop vindicated Cashin. It gave him added encouragement. He became a good debater and never lost an opportunity to condemn the actions of his former leader and close associates in the Bond government. His principal conflicts in the House were with the Liberal leader, Sir Robert Bond, the Honourable E.M. Jackman, and Dr., later Sir, William Lloyd. The official opposition at that time was composed of A.B. Morine, Captain Charley Dawe, Sydney Blandford and another whose name I forget. I think it can be truly said that A.B. Morine was the most outstanding debater the legislature had ever had. He was a great speaker and he, too, like my father, had been in constant conflict with the Honourable E.M. Jackman, who was really a child in his hands. Sir Robert Bond, the Prime Minister, was a great orator, but he was no match for Morine when it came down to debating matters generally, and legislation in particular. Captain Charley Dawe was an outstanding business man from Bay Roberts. He, too, knew the general business of the country, being one of the largest exporters of Labrador fish in those days. He was also aggressive in debate. Between the small Opposition and the Independent member for Ferryland they gave the government of the day many sleepless political nights.

My father was now independent financially. His business at Cape Broyle had made good progress. He had made considerable money on the salvage of wrecks and wrecked goods. A whale factory had been established on the south side of Cape Broyle Harbour. A

Norwegian firm controlled by Eleffsen Brothers had already begun whaling operations out of Aquaforte and were making good profits. This induced my father to interest Bowring Brothers in the building of the Cape Broyle factory, as well as another plant in Hawkes Harbour on the Labrador. Bowring's were the controlling shareholders, but they looked to my father for his guidance in the handling of men and the supplying of the Cape Broyle plant with food and other essentials. He had an investment in this venture of some two thousand dollars. In addition, another company established a plant adjoining the Cape Broyle factory to handle the whale carcasses and bones as well as to extract additional oil from these carcasses and manufacture fertilizer. This latter company was controlled by one Dr. Rismuller, a German, whose proud boast at that time was that he had sat next to Kaiser Wilhelm at college in Germany. Dr. Rismuller was a brilliant man, a great personal friend of my family and he was most courteous and kind to me when I went to Victoria, B.C., in 1912. Rismuller had a patent on the drier for the manufacture of fertilizer.

The whaling business in the latter part of the past century and the early part of the present century was booming in Newfoundland. It was started by that progressive firm of Harvey & Co., Ltd., about the year 1898 and the profits were so huge that it encouraged others to speculate in the industry. Many plants were started in various parts of the Island. Father promoted his own company with Mr. W.C. Job, Tasker Cook, Harry Bowring and others in the riverhead of St. Mary's. The business was over-expanded and finally the demand for the product of this industry declined. It was said that so many whaling steamers were operating off different parts of the Newfoundland coast that they were responsible for driving the whales away from our waters. Ultimately, the business generally folded up and those interested, including my father, lost their investments. Dr. Rismuller then moved to the Pacific coast and, together with Captain Balcom, of Halifax, established several factories along the western seaboard of Canada and the United States. Scores of our Newfoundlanders were brought out to the

Pacific to work on these factories and after a couple or more years returned with considerable money saved. Rismuller and Balcom eventually sold out their interests to the financial syndicate of McKenzie and Mann, familiarly known through the Dominion of Canada as "Bill and Dan." They were the two financial geniuses who promoted the construction of the trans-Canada railway known as the Canadian Northern Railway. They built this railway to compete with the Canadian Pacific. It was located in new, undeveloped country to the north of the C.P.R. Finally, they went bankrupt, and the system had to be taken over by the Canadian government, and with other railroads like the Grand Trunk and the Grand Trunk Pacific, were merged and are now known as the Canadian National Railways. The Newfoundland railway now forms part of that organization.

The Cashin business at Cape Broyle was now expanding. The fisheries were always fairly prosperous. At the outset, the whaling business was a great source of employment and the revenues from the supplies added to the normal profits of the ever-expanding Cape Broyle enterprise. My father spent considerable time away from home. In the summer time, he was either at wrecks, or at the whale factory which had been established at St. Mary's and in which he had the controlling interest. During the winter the legislature was usually in session, and M.P. Cashin, who had become a prominent figure in public life, particularly in his fearless fighting of the Bond government, because of its policy of prohibiting the American bank fishermen from taking bait and supplies on our coast, was now a man with a political future. My father always contended that the business from one American banking vessel was equivalent to the business obtainable from four Nova Scotia vessels. The Opposition members of the legislature, although few in numbers, were big in stature. They were really fighting, patriotic Newfoundlanders. In this category I do not include Mr. Morine, as he was not a Newfoundlander. Nothing of a contentious character in the way of legislation was introduced into the House, which did not receive the closest scrutiny and many times, the condemnation of the Independent member from Ferryland. Cashin had now made up his mind that he had a political future and concentrated his efforts in this direction.

During the sessions of the House of Assembly and other occasions as well, my father was a constant visitor to the home of P. T. McGrath, later Sir Patrick McGrath, who at that time was Clerk of the House, as well as being editor of the *Daily Herald*. McGrath was one of those who was working on the inside track to sponsor Sir Edward Morris as leader of a new party to oppose the Bond government at the next general election. Morris, although attorney general at that time, and shrewd politician that he was, did not enter into any conflict with either my father or the other members of the Opposition on any contentious matter. He was watching for the opportune moment to break from Bond and lead his own party. Another person who was a constant visitor to the McGrath home during that time was the late Judge George Emerson, who had been a member of the House of Assembly in former years, and who was now quietly working to dethrone Bond. Judge Emerson was vindictive towards Bond because he was not made Chief Justice of the Supreme Court on the death of Judge J.I. Little in 1902. This important position was given to the late Chief Justice, Sir William Horwood. Emerson was an advocate of Morris to lead a new party, and one might say, was actually prostituting his position as a judge of the Supreme Court.

While all these things were going on and M. P. Cashin was away from Cape Broyle, his wife, Gertrude Cashin, was the mainstay of the commercial business at home. She worked like a slave and had the peculiar knack of being able to get others to work hard without ever appearing to be dictatorial in her attitudes. The men always called her the "Mistress" and father "the Boss." As a result of these activities, our house at Cape Broyle, which at first was very small, was enlarged. The roof was raised to make room for extra maids and children. An addition was made to supply eating quarters for the trap crews and other men working around the premises. Mother supervised all this work personally. The business premises, once a mere stage-head and an old shop and store, were also expanded.

I had now been practically planted at Cape Broyle, and was not permitted to spend any of my summer holidays at Witless Bay. Efforts were being made to eradicate my connections with my affectionate old Grandmother Mullowney. That was an absolute impossibility. Even now, as I write these memoirs, I still look upon Grandmother Mullowney as the one person who really cared for me, who reared me from infancy to when I was slowly brought to Cape Broyle to work at all kinds of labour, from the carrying of the fish-barrow, the rowing of the bow oar of a trap skiff during the summer, the salting of fish, the chasing of Nova Scotia vessels for business, to the handling of blubber and oil. It was a special privilege to be permitted to tend the store. My physical condition was perfect. To use a common expression of that time, "I was as strong as a bull." I could handle a barrel of flour or pork with ease. I felt proud that I was able to do it. I could hoist a tub of salt out of the hold of a western boat or freighter. At all times I lived in deadly fear of my father, who, no matter how hard I worked or how well I did the job, was always critical of my actions, and who, even before I left school in 1906, drove me, during my so-called holidays, harder than any man in his service.

I was doing fairly well in school at St. Bonaventure's College and in 1905 passed my Intermediate Grade fairly successfully. Latin was my most difficult subject. To be frank, I detested that subject. I do not believe that if I had continued there for another ten years, I could have mastered the subject with any degree of success. I returned to school again in September, 1905, and was put in Associate Grade after the results of the C.H.E. examinations had been made public and I had passed Intermediate. Associate Grade at that time, I am now informed, was the equivalent of eleventh grade today. During these five or six years at St. Bon's I had, as teachers, such outstanding men as Brothers Fennessy, Daly, Lannon, Ryan, Prendergast and finally, Brother Culhane, who had been appointed Brother Superior, succeeding Brother Downey a couple of years previously. I had never had the privilege of being in the class of Brother Downey, who was the principal of the college for the first few years I attended that institution. All these reverend gentlemen were outstanding masters in the field of education at that time. St. Bonaventure's College generally led the island in the annual C.H.E. examinations in competition with the other colleges. Our school was awarded the first Rhodes scholarship through Sydney Herbert, the second was awarded to Bert Bond, nephew of Sir Robert Bond, and, as I have already related, the third went to my old friend, John Penney. St. Bon's also, at that time, was foremost in athletics, particularly in cricket and football. Later they developed in the mastery of ice hockey.

I continued in Associate Grade until sometime in March, 1906, when, one Sunday, my father arrived at the college and informed Brother Superior Culhane that he was taking me away from school, and putting me to work as a junior office boy in Bowring's office on April 1st, 1906. If I were superstitious I would say, "What a day to face the world in any branch of activity." That ended my education. I was supposed to be fully equipped to face the world with all its "ups and downs," its trials and tribulations, with no more than a tenth grade education. There was never any talk at home or elsewhere as to whether or not I was suited for a profession, or whether or not I was desirous of acquiring further qualifications in the field of education. I had nothing whatever to say about such matters. I had to do just as I was told to do by father or mother. Two other of my brothers were now boarding students at the college, a considerable financial strain at that time for my parents. Larry had been living in the United States with my Aunt Jane Mullowney for his health, which was always poor. My late brother, Dick, then about twelve years old, was also a boarding student. I, being the oldest of the family, had now to embark in the hurly burly of life. Father had lost considerable of the money he had made on wrecks, in paying the back debts of his brother, speculating in whale factories, and building up Cape Broyle. He was still independent financially. His strong ambitions for public office necessitated the expenditure of additional money, but he was determined to hold public office and be a Cabinet minister in a new government. This ambition overcrowded everything else in his life. There was no more theoretical education for me. I was now barely sixteen years old.

Chapter 2

I Begin Work
And Face The World

On the afternoon of March 31st, 1906, my father was in St. John's attending the regular sessions of the House of Assembly. As I related in the previous chapter, he had made arrangements whereby I would be employed as junior clerk in the office of Messrs. Bowring Bros., Ltd. So, on that Sunday afternoon of March 31st, father came to the college and took me down to live with an old and respected cousin of his on Prescott Street. This dear old lady's name was Mrs. Anne Morris, formerly a Fennelly from Fermeuse. Her mother and my father's mother were sisters. This was where I was to board for the next five or six months. Father gave Mrs. Morris instructions as to what I was to do when I was not actually working at the office. I was ordered to go to mass every morning. I was not to be out of the house after ten o'clock at night. I had been fitted out with the necessary clothing, etc., all of which was paid for by my father. The late Robert Johnson, the tailor, made me a couple of suits of clothes, knickerbocker pants, from the finest material which father had salvaged out of one of the many wrecked vessels he had handled in those days. I had not yet been permitted to wear long trousers. They were not the style at that time for boys of my age.

If my memory serves me correctly, I was brought down to Bowring's office on Monday morning, April 1st, 1906, by my father and introduced to Mr. F. W. Hayward, who at that time was cashier and, in a way, office manager of the Bowring Company. I was then put to work and shown what I was to do. Really, the first few days I did practically nothing except run messages for Mr. Hayward. Gradually, I was trained in the changing of the various store books each evening. The system was entirely different than it is today. I was introduced to Mr. Edgar R. Bowring, who was the managing director of the entire Bowring business in

Newfoundland. He was the same gentleman who gave my father the opportunity of starting his Cape Broyle business just twenty years earlier. I was also introduced to Mr. Henry A. Bowring, brother of Mr. Edgar and father of Edgar R. Bowring, Jr., later one of the heads of this vast Bowring Corporation in the United Kingdom. Then I was to meet Mr. John S. Munn, stepson of Mr. Edgar Bowring, who had been taken into the firm and later became managing director. Mr. Munn and his little daughter were drowned when the ill-fated *Florizel* was stranded near Cappahayden in the early part of 1918. Mr. Munn was a real gentleman and, in my opinion, Newfoundland lost one of her most outstanding commercial men when Jack Munn was drowned. Then I was taken in to meet Mr. F.W. Rennie, who was really the head of all the office staff. Mr. Rennie was the uncle of both Mr. Edgar Bowring and Mr. Henry Bowring. The other members of the office staff at that time were Mr. William C. Collins, who was second bookkeeper, the late Bob Simms, James T. Foley, now deceased, who later became manager of the government coastal system, when that service was taken over from Bowrings by the government in 1919, Fred Hayward, Jr., and Billy Caldwell, later in the insurance business in St. John's. At that time, the entire staff of the office and stores consisted of men. There was not one lady working in either the office or stores. That situation prevailed in nearly all stores and offices of the various mercantile firms doing business along Water Street at that time.

Really, I cannot honestly say that I was sorry to leave school at that time. I should say that, if I had been given the choice of staying at college or going to Bowring's, I would have chosen the latter. In my subconscious mind, I no doubt felt that I would have certain freedoms when I went to work which I could not have at school. I felt that I would be a great business man over night and that Mr. Bowring himself would soon be looking to me for a job. I wanted to be free to go and come when I liked, to do what I liked, and no doubt I felt that I could take general charge of everything. I was to find out my mistake in that respect before many days had passed.

At that time the firm of Bowring Brothers paid their

employees monthly in advance. When I started to work that Monday morning, I did not know what salary I was to get, but much to my surprise, about eleven a.m., Mr. Hayward called me and said, "Peter, today is pay-day," and I received the munificent sum of ten dollars which was to be my monthly salary for a period of twelve months. I did not have a cent in my pocket, and ten dollars looked like a fortune to me. What was I to do with this money? For the previous couple of years at St. Bonaventure's College I had been smoking, and, yes, chewing tobacco. Many other boys were doing likewise. So, together with Billy Caldwell, I went down to Cash's Tobacco Store and bought a pipe which cost around two dollars and a plug of Master Workman tobacco. I now felt that I was a real man of the world. I went home to Mrs. Morris' to dinner and returned to work about 2 p.m. With one of the other young boys of the office, I think it was Percy LeMessurier, I was brought around the various stores in the evening about five p.m., and shown how the day books were to be changed every day at this hour. I came to know the heads or managers of the various stores. All these men knew my father and mother, because they had been doing business with the Bowring firm for about twenty years. Mr. Walter Wills was manager of the retail store. Mr. John LeMessurier was manager of the hardware and grocery stores, whilst Mr. Grieve was manager of the dry goods store. Later I was to get to know Mr. R. B. Crocker, who was wharfmaster of the north side premises, Mr. Ira S. Kennedy, manager of the south side premises and the late councillor John P. Kelly, manager of the Mudge's premises in the west end. Also, "Dicky" Ash, as we all called him, was in charge of the operation of the two coastal boats, *Portia* and *Prospero,* and his assistant, Mr. Hugh LeMessurier, later manager of the Standard Manufacturing Company, Ltd. All these gentlemen were most generous and kind to me.

When I returned to my boarding house at Mrs. Morris' the evening of April 1st, I stayed around after supper talking with both Mr. and Mrs. Morris. Father came in there that night. He had known that we were paid that day. The first thing he asked was, was I paid today? I said, "Yes." "How much did you get?" he enquired. I told him ten dollars. "What did you do with the money?" I then told him I had bought a pipe, some tobacco and, I think, a couple of packages of Gem cigarettes. He was more than annoyed. Whatever money I had left out of that huge amount of ten dollars, he ordered me to hand over to him. I did this. "In future," my father told me, "your ten dollars per month salary will be sent to me. Your board has to be paid." I think my board and lodging at that time was fifteen dollars per month. This action on father's part left me financially stranded, whilst, in addition, he took the pipe and tobacco from me. The following day he instructed Mr. Hayward to forward my ten dollar a month salary to him (father) personally, whilst he told Mrs. Morris to let me have one dollar each week as pocket money.

Maybe I deserved this disciplinary action on my father's part, but it left a feeling of strong resentment in my system, whilst, in addition, members of the office staff, who knew of this action, continually brought it to my attention. It certainly created a strong feeling of resentment in my mental system, which gave me an inferiority complex. My father did not feel that boys of my age should begin to smoke at such an early period of their lives. Nevertheless, this action on his part did not deter me from having the occasional cigarette. At that time there was a small store on the corner of Prescott and Gower Streets, where one could buy two cigarettes for just barely one cent. And so, on each occasion that I would receive that allowance of one dollar per week from that charming old lady, Mrs. Morris, the first place I went to was Miss Walsh's store just across the street to purchase a few cigarettes. In addition, some boys of around my age and a little older were generous and kind enough to pass me the occasional "fag." Many of them sneered at me, because they all knew the regulations laid down by my father as to my future conduct. This, too, had considerable effect on my mental system which took me years to overcome.

I carried out father's instructions to that lovable Mrs. Morris to the best of my ability. There were many occasions, particularly when father was not in town, that I did not carry out his rigid instructions to the letter. From a religious standpoint, I do not think that these particular orders did me much good, although I was strong on the principle of doing my church duties regularly. This had been instilled in my mind by the good Irish Christian Brothers during the six years I attended St. Bonaventure's College. These little pieces of disobedience on my part were covered up by. Mrs. Morris. However, when father came to town he always checked up on me as to what I was doing in off hours. In one particular instance, a certain person took pleasure in tattling on me, even though my actions were of a boyish, frivolous character. This particular individual was a strong political supporter of father's public attitudes and was looking forward to an appointment in the government service when a change of national administration took place. This same gentleman later went into business for himself, failed, and was finally appointed by my father to an outport position in the customs department. I do not hold any grudge against this particular individual because of his actions. He undoubtedly felt in his own mind that he was acting in the best interest of my future success. It is coincidental, however, that some twenty-three years later I, as Minister of Finance and Customs of Newfoundland, was primarily responsible for having this gentleman receive his legitimate pension, which he had been deprived of by the previous government. We became great personal friends and I showed no vindictiveness towards him.

During the month of April, 1906, I was being gradually educated in my position as junior office boy. My duties were being defined daily and I was becoming familiar with the general office routine. Each morning I was to be at the office not later than nine o'clock, open the safes, have the journals and ledgers on the bookkeepers' desks. The bills, or to use the modern term, invoices, would be mailed to the outports and those in the city would be delivered by hand. We also had a senior messenger in the office by the name of Charley Adey, whose duty it was to deliver bills in certain parts of the city, whilst I, the junior boy, had to deliver the bills and accounts to the various firms on

Water Street. Then at the end of each month, the monthly accounts or statements for the various Water Street and other St. John's firms had to be delivered and I was assigned the job of delivering and collecting the money for these accounts. I generally spent the forenoon part of the day doing this work; and to be honest, not alone with myself, but my readers and former employers, I have to admit there were times I loafed on the job. In general, I became acquainted quickly with my various duties and before the end of April, 1906, was progressing favourably.

During the month of April the sealers would be generally returning from the sealfishery. At that time the firm of Bowring Brothers had some six or seven ships prosecuting this industry, and when these vessels returned, either with or without a paying cargo, it created further work for the office staff. Two sealing masters stand out prominently in my mind as I write these memoirs. The first, and I would say the most colourful of Newfoundland sealing skippers, was the then well-known Captain Arthur Jackman. He was captain of the S.S. *Eagle* during the 1906 season, but, unfortunately, did not have his usual good fortune that year. Captain Jackman was a great personal friend of my father's and for several years before his death had given Mike Cashin, as he called him, some thirty berths to the ice in the *Eagle* for fishermen from the district of Ferryland. This 1906 voyage to the frozen icefields was the last that the old "Scorcher" (Captain Jackman) ever made. Arthur Jackman was highly thought of by the Bowring firm, particularly by the heads of the corporation in England. With them, Captain Arthur Jackman could do no wrong. He had many successful trips to the sealfishery, was fortunate in never losing a man, whilst he looked after his owners' interests in every respect. In addition to being master of one of Bowring's sealing ships, Captain Jackman was also ship's husband or marine superintendent and supervised the repair and general upkeep of all the Bowring sealing steamers and coastal steamers. In fact Arthur Jackman was part of the Bowring corporation. He came from a traditionally sea-faring family. His brother, Captain William Jackman, is the great

Newfoundlander who saved some twenty-seven or twenty-nine lives in the 1870s on the Labrador coast, by swimming back and forth some twenty seven times from a stranded vessel, each time carrying one of the members of the wrecked ship on his back through the surging waves to safety. It is questionable if the equal of such a heroic deed has ever been performed in the annals of the sea, either in Newfoundland or elsewhere.

The Jackman family had its roots in Renews, one of the finest fishing settlements in Newfoundland. There are some of their descendents still living there, whilst other relatives or distant relatives now reside in St. John's West, and in nearly every case they are imbued with the desire for avocation with the sea. It would not be proper to close this particular reference to Captain Arthur Jackman without relating one incident, a true story of the courage and fearlessness of this outstanding Newfoundland seaman. On one of Jackman's voyages to the sealfishery he accidentally maimed one of his fingers in operating one of the ship's winches. He knew this finger would have to be amputated. He immediately ordered his chief engineer to bring along an axe and to cut it off. The engineer did not have the nerve to perform this operation, so Jackman took the axe himself, laid the wounded hand on the rail of the vessel and chopped off the finger himself. And again, when Arthur Jackman was dying during the winter of 1907, his nephew, the late Reverend Father William Jackman administered the last rites of Catholic church to his courageous uncle. When the last sacrament had been given him and absolution granted, the old Scorcher (Captain Jackman), true to his traditions, uttered his last words, which again showed his fearlessness. These words were: "put the flags on her, Billy boy, and let her go. Give my clothes to Mick Maddigan." Maddigan had always been his boatswain on his many sealing and whaling voyages. He was familiarly known as the "Ruffian" and went by the name of "Ruffian Maddigan."

Then another outstanding sealing master sailing under the Bowring flag at that time, for years previous as well as many years afterwards, was Captain Abraham Kean. Captain Kean passed away in 1945 at the ripe old age of ninety. He had been master of sealing steamers to the sealfishery for fifty years and during that period carried in to the port of St. John's over one million seals, or an average of twenty thousand each year. This is the record both in years as master and in quantities of seals obtained by any of our Newfoundland sealing skippers. Captain Kean was not as colourful as Captain Jackman and there was no love lost between these two mariners. In addition to being a sealing skipper, Captain Kean was also master of the Bowring coastal steamer, *Prospero,* which was one of the ships under contract to the Newfoundland government at that time to service the north east coast of the island during the summer months. He also conducted a fishing business at Brookfield on the north side of Bonavista Bay. During the last couple of years in World War One, Kean invested his money in a couple of foreign-going sailing vessels and when the "slump" came in 1919-20 he lost both the vessels and his money. Nevertheless, this old gentleman carried on. He became a broker and auctioneer in St. John's and still continued his annual sealing voyages as master of various Bowring sealing vessels. Captain Kean was also keenly interested in the public life of the island and was at one time a member of our local Parliament. Eventually, in 1924-25, he became a member of our Upper House or Legislative Council.

It did not take me very long to become friends with all members of the staff, both in the office, the stores and the wharf. I became friends with the fish cullers, the watchmen, the engineers on the various ships, the old skipper of the little harbour tug, *Zelda,* whose name was Bill White, and also the engineer of that little tug, Bill Squires. On numerous occasions I would go down on the north side wharf, particularly at nights and Sundays. I would talk with these men. They were all noble characters. They were all kind to me. Oh, how I enjoyed having a mug of tea with either one of the watchmen, Tom Brien or Andy Walsh. I remember that big old black dog of Tom Brien's which he called "Tatters." Tatters was a mongrel breed, was certainly a great watch-dog; and nothing of an unusual character could occur around that premise, which Tatters did not detect.

At that time in the history of business in St. John's as

well as in other parts of the island, great activity prevailed during the months of April, May and June. Hundreds, yes, thousands of fishermen planters and fishermen came to St. John's to procure supplies from the various merchants in order to prosecute the cod-fishery. The small harbour of St. John's was literally crowded with vessels, schooners, western boats and jacks, from nearly every part of the country. Bowring's at that time were one of the largest, if not the largest supplying firms for the fishing industry. Their various wharves were bristling with activity. Outport merchants had their vessels or schooners waiting to get alongside to load their goods for the summer. Fishermen and sharemen from the north, south, south-west coast and even from the Straits of Belle Isle were arranging for their outfits, for the purpose of carrying out what was then Newfoundland's greatest and most valuable industry. The shops, stores and offices all along Water Street were open each night during the spring months in order to service these various dealers and their crews. There was no such thing as loafing on the job during that season. The clerks in the various stores would be filling the orders placed through the office and the clerks in the office would be attending to the making out of bills or invoices for the various dealers, their sharemen or crews. There was no such thing as a clerks' union even dreamed of. Everyone worked when the boss ordered him to work and there was no such thing as being paid overtime. The clerks were lucky to have jobs, and to hold those jobs, they had to work. The boss, and not the union, was the dictator. Mercantile offices were frequently open when the stores were closed, particularly in the spring and autumn seasons. Crowds of outport planters and fishermen would be found on Water Street during these particular periods. The office had to remain open to serve the outport planters and their sharemen with bills or invoices covering their supplies.

Whilst as a youth I did not relish this sort of night work, it served to give me experience which helped me considerably as years passed. In the meantime, for the first couple of months of my entry into the business life of the country as a junior clerk, I became acquainted with other boys of my age or maybe a little older, who were members of clubs or societies in the city. I was able to persuade my father to permit me to join the Benevolent Irish Society and he paid my fee. This was, then, a place for me to go after my work. I became acquainted with nearly all the young members as well as the senior members of the Society. They were all very friendly and kind towards me. However, the rule was laid down for me that I was not to be out of my boarding house after 10 p.m., and again Mrs. Morris was advised accordingly. I am afraid I did not carry out this parental regulation to the letter. I learned to play the game of billiards. I enjoyed this gentlemanly recreation very much indeed. I also learned to play cards. Sometimes I did not have the money to play with, if by chance I lost the game, but nevertheless it was not very difficult in those days to finance such an amusement. The club closed every night at eleven o'clock, and I was nearly always there when its doors were locked. I had to take a chance on the kindness of Mrs. Morris not to report my actions in this respect when father came to town. I took too many of these chances, because even though Mrs. Morris covered me up on all occasions, there were others who were only too glad to have the opportunity of tattling on me regarding my being out of the house after ten o'clock at night, for playing cards, not only in the club rooms but in other places, for small amounts of money, as well as committing other misdemeanors which were not unusual for boys of my age.

During the summer months of 1906, we worked in the offices and the stores during the days, having the usual one hour for dinner, or as it is called today, lunch. There was no night work. In addition we had a half holiday on Wednesday afternoons and one Wednesday each month was a whole holiday. However, we were kept busy during the day time, as there were always orders coming from the outports to ship goods by the coastal boats to the various outport dealers. Also, many of the outport dealers, planters or merchants operated their own coasting schooners or boats, which were continually coming to St. John's for additional supplies of all kinds. The bills or invoices for such goods had to be made out and ready for the first mail, or delivered by hand immediately the goods were shipped.

That particular summer, I became interested in the senior football games in St. John's, very rarely missing a football match, particularly between the Star and Benevolent Irish Society teams. Whilst the B.I.S. should have been the team I ordinarily would have given my support, I, like many other members of that great Irish society, felt that a most unsportsmanlike trick had been played by the Irish on the Star team. At these particular games we showed our enthusiasm in no uncertain manner by cheering and encouraging the Star team. When that great old Star team won the championship that season, I remember distinctly the great crowds that gathered around the Star players and finally carried the late Jim Vinicombe, the captain and leader of that historic team on their shoulders from St. George's field to the Star Hall, where the late E.M. Jackman, then President of the Star of the Sea Society, complimented all those responsible for the great success of the Star team. Little did I think at that time that, less than twenty years later, I was to become President of that grand old society, an office I held continuously for a period of twelve years, when I retired and became honorary president.

It was also during the summer of 1906 that the first walking match was held in the city. Bob Simms, who was in charge of the insurance department in our office, was one of the favourite contenders. Many of us followed the walkers around the full twenty mile course, doing everything we could in the way of encouragement, to help Bob hold the lead he had from the start. However, the race was won by the late J.W. Morris, whilst the late Bert Hayward and the late Bob Simms were close up to Mr. Morris. I also in 1906 attended my first Regatta, which is held annually on Quidi Vidi Lake, and had the usual keen interest in that Newfoundland Derby Day. Mother came to town frequently on business and I was always fortunate in being able to get the occasional dollar or two from her as pocket money. Honestly, I do not know how I would have been able to hold my place with the other young working boys without mother's generous financial assistance. Even in those days, one could not get far on an allowance of one dollar per week.

Then the month of September, 1906, came around. It was about this time that the new salt codfish began to come in; and vessels and boats carrying Shore, Labrador and Straits fish were coming to St. John's consigned to the various merchants and merchant firms, who had outfitted them for Newfoundland's main industry. Offices, shops and stores were open at night time and the firm of Bowring Brothers, Ltd. was one of the outstanding firms buying and shipping these fishery products. All employees, both in offices and stores, were kept unusually busy. In addition to the six sealing ships and two coastal boats being operated by the Bowring company at that time, the firm also operated three foreign-going sailing vessels. These ships were used to carry salt codfish, seal oil and seal skins to the European markets as well as to the West Indies and Brazilian markets. They generally had return cargoes of salt and molasses. I remember the names of these three sailing vessels. There was the barque *Cordelia*, under the command of Captain Taylor, the *Dunure*, whose master came from Cape Broyle in the person of Captain Edward Hartery, and the steel vessel, *Margaret Murray*, in charge of Captain J.R. Williams, a Welshman, who later went with the Red Cross Line controlled by the Bowring firm, then became master of the S.S. *Rosalind* running on the St. John's-Montreal route. Finally Captain Williams was transferred to one of the many ships owned and operated by the parent company of C.T. Bowring & Company, Ltd., of Liverpool, England.

My duties at this time were the compilation of the receipts for the fish from the various dealers, planters or outport merchants. First the fish had to be landed from the several vessels, schooners or boats, culled by specially sworn cullers, tallied by a special tallyman and each evening the tallyman came to the office and gave in his returns to Jim Foley, who had charge of the large fish book. This book gave the names, the quantities in quintals of the various qualities of fish received from each dealer or fisherman, as the case may be. When the receipts were made out and each quality priced by one of the Messrs. Bowring, the total values were extended and checked. Then, following this procedure, the original receipts were mailed or delivered to the individual merchant dealers or sharemen. The fish book, together with the copies of the receipts, was handed to the two bookkeepers who credited the amounts to the accounts of the outport merchants and sharemen. This entire procedure involved a lot of work and was generally done during the night working hours. Both myself and Percy LeMessurier worked hard at this particular job, because we wanted to have it done early. The rules were that the office would close at 9:30 p.m. It was very seldom that I got away from that office before 10 p.m., or even later. Mr. Rennie, the chief bookkeeper, very rarely returned from supper before 8 p.m., and was not particularly quick in doing his job. It was the duty of the junior clerk (me), to wait to put all the ledgers and journals in the safe when the bookkeepers had finished their day's work. In this respect, how often, I wonder, did I take poor old Mr. Rennie's books off his desk around 8:30 or 9 p.m., when he had not returned from supper, only to have the poor old gentleman turn up a little later and order me to get the books out of the safe. I received many reprimands from this charming old gentleman, who developed into a great personal friend of mine years later, when he had retired, and I returned from the First World War and entered the public life of the country. I frequently met him on Water Street in the summer afternoons, when he was taking his customary walk, and at times reminded him of those days, when he hauled me "over the coals." William Collins was not so strict with me when he was second bookkeeper. Mr. Rennie was always cranky and unpleasant when he tried to draw a trial balance each month. Invariably he was unable to get his books to balance properly. Then he generally called on Jim Foley to come to his rescue. Foley was a clever chap at this sort of work, and as I recall now, I can hear Mr. Rennie call "James," as he addressed Foley, and ask him to try and find his errors.

Foley was generally able, after some considerable investigation, to get Mr. Rennie's books to balance properly. Yes, and on occasions he gave Jim Foley five or ten dollars for helping him out.

When Christmas came around in 1906, father asked Mr. Hayward if I could go home to Cape Broyle for a few days to spend the festive season. I thought this was kind on his part. He wanted to have all the family together, if at all possible, for this annual celebration. It was during this short visit, at Christmas, 1906, that mother gave me a present of a season ticket to the Princess rink, which entitled me to go there skating each night there was no hockey game. This thoughtfulness on mother's part enabled me to join with other boys and girls of my age in this great recreation. I enjoyed every moment of the times spent there, when myself and my first girl friend, Phil O'Driscoll, skated out many of the bands each night; and how I enjoyed taking her home to her house on Bond Street and carrying her skates on my shoulder. We were both very young and shy about our parents knowing of our innocent flirtation. Well do I remember there was some game on in the Princess rink, when Phil, as she was called, and I were walking around the rink together during the intermission. Who did we butt into but father and the late Captain Tom Bonia. We immediately turned around and ran the other way, much to their enjoyment. The first time I met Captain Bonia a few days later he remarked; "I see you are going around with a Mobile goat." The O'Driscolls came from Mobile originally and the saying goes, that at one time a "goat spoke in Mobile." From that time onwards the people in that settlement were called Mobile goats.

I returned to the office after New Year, 1907, having enjoyed my few days holidays back in Cape Broyle. I drove over the road by horse and sleigh, and, it is needless to say, was charmed to see my dear old Grandmother Mullowney, whom I loved so dearly. She felt proud of me then, even though I was just a junior clerk in the great Bowring firm, receiving that munificent salary of ten dollars per month.

It was early in the winter of 1907 that Captain Arthur

Jackman, whom I have already referred to in this chapter, passed to his eternal reward. He died at the home of his nephew, the late councillor John P. Kelly, who had charge of Bowring's west end premises, known as Mudge's. Captain Jackman's funeral was the largest I have ever seen. People in all walks of life followed the bier of the old "Scorcher" to its last resting place in Belvedere cemetery. Bowring's entire establishment was closed for the day out of respect to that great Newfoundland mariner. How often, I wonder, did Mr. Edgar Bowring ring that bell for the junior clerk, and how quickly did I answer that call, to have Mr. Bowring say to me in that commanding and autocratic manner: "Peter, go up to Strang's and tell Captain Jackman I want to see him immediately." I, eager as I was to carry out Mr. Bowring's orders, always ran at full speed to Strang's liquor store, about one hundred yards west of the office on Water Street. I felt privileged to have the opportunity of running in the side door to the back bar and telling that brave soldier of the sea that Mr. Bowring wanted him. At that time I was never even tempted nor did I have the desire to take that alcoholic beverage. But later in this book I will tell some of the part alcohol has played in my hectic life.

Shortly after Captain Jackman's death, preparations began again for the prosecution of the sealfishery for the 1907 venture. I believe this was the year of the advent of the steel ships. If my memory serves me correctly, the firm of A. Harvey & Co., Ltd., organized and incorporated a new company known as the Adventure Steamship Co., Ltd. This company had a special ship built in the United Kingdom for the prosecution of this important industry. The ship was built of steel, was much larger and faster than any of the oldtime wooden vessels. The name of this particular ship was the *Adventure* and she was under the command of Captain Henry Dawe for the first few years she went to the ice. During the summer the vessel was generally chartered to outside shipping companies, whilst she was also profitably employed in the carrying of coal from Sydney to St. John's. I remember the preparations for that particular sealing venture of 1907.

Over twenty ships carrying between three and four thousand men took part in the seal hunt. Six or maybe seven of these ships were operated under the Bowring colours. I distinctly remember the signing of the various Bowring crews a few days before March the 10th, the sailing date, the fitting out of the sealers with their "crop" or advance of some nine or twelve dollars. This "crop" or advance consisted mainly of sealskin boots for each of the crew, some tobacco, oatmeal, sugar and raisins and some other necessities of comfort. The actual cost was nine dollars, but in view of the fact that the firm was taking a gamble on the venture, the sealers were charged twelve dollars or $33\frac{1}{3}\%$ more than the actual cost. In those days, it cost an average of between twelve and fifteen thousand dollars to fit out one of these wooden steamers for the great adventure.

I remember the morning of March the 10th, 1907, the morning arranged for the sailing of the sealing fleet. There were thousands of people lining the wharves along the north side waterfront, whilst hundreds more went to Signal Hill to witness the spectacular sailing of the ships through the St. John's Narrows. By noon that same day all the ships were out of sight and people were praying for the success of the venture. It was customary, in fact it was an unwritten law, that several sweepstakes would be held either for the "first arrival," or the total number of seals killed for the season. Nearly everyone bought tickets and everyone was speculating on his or her ship being the first arrival from the frozen icefields. Then the rumors would start - rumors that the *Eagle* or some other ship had passed Cape Bonavista with all flags flying, homeward bound. There was no wireless telegraphy in those days. Finally the first ship, lucky enough to hit the "main patch" early, would arrive back in St. John's around the last few days in March. Then the flipper suppers would be all the rage. These were what we called the "good old days." They are now, like "Clementine", "lost and gone for ever." Let us hope we are passing through a much happier period. For me, I doubt it.

The general annual total catch of seals in those days was upwards of three hundred thousand and, as already related, between three and four thousand men comprised the crews of the sealing ships. These men invariably came from the northern part of the island, principally the north side of Bonavista Bay. Apart from the few berths which father was able to scrounge off Bowring's or some of the captains, there were a small number from the Southern Shore. I was one of the clerks from the Bowring office, who helped call the roll the morning of the sailing. If some member of the crew did not turn up, and invariably there were a few firemen missing, it was not difficult to find a man to take his place. The individual volunteer generally went as he stood. It was called a "pier-head jump." He took chances on being able to get some additional clothing on board the ship. It was a wonderful sight, to see these old wooden sealing ships back off from their respective wharves and straighten out, with all flags flying to pass through the St. John's Narrows. Cheers from the spectators could be heard all along the waterfront, the ships' whistles were blowing and the members of the various crews were waving their caps and cheering to the land-lubbers. It was indeed a wonderful sight. There is nothing like it today.

That particular spring (1907) saw some changes in the Bowring sealing skippers, which was primarily caused through the death of Captain Arthur Jackman . Captain Edward Bishop was given charge of the *Ranger*. Captain Bishop also conducted a most successful fishing business at Wesleyville and was one of nature's gentlemen. Captain Joe Kean, son of Captain Abraham Kean, who had been master of the *Ranger* the previous year, was given charge of the *Eagle*. I became great friends of all these fine Newfoundlanders. I remember Captain Danny Greene, of Newtown, who was master of the *Aurora* and who prosecuted the Labrador fishery in the summer season with his own schooner. Two days before the sailing of the *Aurora,* which was my seventeenth birthday, I took a few of my young friends down aboard that ship to meet Captain Greene. His hospitality to us was unequalled to anything I have experienced. Those young men certainly enjoyed themselves and drank several toasts to

Captain Greene, wishing him every success in the forthcoming seal hunt. I consumed an unusual amount of ginger ale, but later got into my usual trouble with my father when he heard from someone how I passed my time on that particular Sunday afternoon. These various boyish troubles in which I was continuously involving myself, were building themselves up for a climax which was inevitable, unless I suddenly decided to lead what one might call a junior hermit's life. Poor old Mrs. Morris had been covering me up over what I considered harmless episodes for considerable time, so my father decided to move me out of her house and obtained a place for me to stay with Mrs. Captain Collins, mother of William Collins, our second bookkeeper. Mrs. Collins was another sweet old lady and treated me with every kindness. She too, like Mrs. Morris, closed both her eyes and ears to many of my youthful misdemeanors. That year saw seven of the Bowring sealing ships carry to the port of St. John's around sixty-two thousand seals, and their return from the icefields around the first part of April and later added to our regular office duties.

Following the clearing up of the sealing voyage, we had the usual repetition experienced each spring season of stores and offices being open at night for the purpose of supplying the outport merchants, planters and fishermen for the prosecution of the 1907 cod-fishery. These activities were really a "hardy annual." It meant seeing again faces of men whom you had not laid eyes on since the previous autumn. It was really a renewal of acquaintances -- a getting together of individuals from all sections of the island who had not seen each other for at least six months. It meant the regular routine of orders through the office which had to be approved by the Messrs. Bowring, and the making out of bills or invoices covering these various transactions. It meant the usual additional night work which the junior clerk, because of his position, had to do. It meant the usual effort at night time of trying to get the ledgers and journals stowed away in the safes to get away from the office as early as I could. It meant the usual reprimand from Mr. Rennie for my actions in this respect, actions which in many cases were inspired by senior clerks for the purpose of hearing poor old Mr. Rennie give me a "telling off." Nevertheless, I continued to try and get away with these tactics practically every night the office was open for business. Sometimes, not only did Mr. Rennie administer a sound lecture in the form of a reprimand, but he added to this reprimand some of the usual unprintable names which he applied to me. There were times when my good friend Will Collins would be later at night than Mr. Rennie, but peculiarly enough I did not mind Mr. Collins being late. I enjoyed talking with him and on many occasions when we had the office to ourselves, just the two of us, we would have a private wrestling match with no spectators. Collins was one of the outstanding goalkeepers the old Star football team ever had. He was always in great physical condition, and although he was light in weight, his muscular capabilities were unusual for a man of his size. I could never pin him down, even though I could lift him all over the place. He was too agile a man for me.

During the summer of 1907, now that I had become well acquainted with many other boys of my age or a little older, most of whom were members of the Irish Society, I played cards or billiards whenever possible at night time and on Sundays. Also, there were times during working hours that I went to the club and had a game of billiards. On the occasional Sunday afternoon, I sometimes went out to Donovan's on an excursion train with others and had supper there. Just imagine, one could have a delicious supper at Donovan's in those days for not more than thirty cents. Incidentally, on April 1st, 1907, my salary was raised from ten dollars per month to $13.33 per month. That was a policy of the Bowring firm for the advancement of all junior office boys. In spite of this generous raise in salary, amounting to forty dollars per year, it did not mean that my pocket money allowance per week was increased. My monthly salary, as usual, had to be sent to my father, to go against my board money, which was now twenty dollars per month. Therefore I was no better off financially than when I was earning ten dollars per month.

Somehow or other I was able to find the necessary funds to attend the football games, the hockey games and the Regatta of 1907. Sometime in August or September of 1907, my Aunt Jane Mullowney, who was my godmother, returned from the United States for a holiday to see her mother, Grandmother Mullowney, as well as other relatives, who included my mother, her sister. Aunt Jane was always kind to me when she came back from America for a holiday. Even though I had learned shorthand and typewriting at St. Bonaventure's College, I very seldom was given an opportunity at the Bowring office to show my proficiency in this particular line. However, there was outside work which might be procurable, if one had a machine of his own to do work at night time. Aunt Jane bought me a Smith Premier typewriter for a present before she returned to Bangor, Maine. I think she paid around $120.00 for it. I performed a few small jobs for outsiders and received the customary remuneration for it. I was generally short of pocket money, so, I came to the conclusion that I could raise some extra cash if I sold the typewriter. This I did. For a couple of months neither my father or mother knew that I had disposed of the machine. However, my action in this respect was eventually discovered by father and it made him furious. As I was only seventeen years old at the time, it appears that even though I really owned the typewriter, I could not dispose of it without my parents' permission. I had received $75.00 in cash for the typewriter. Father insisted that the people who purchased it would return it to him which they did, when he repaid the seventy-five dollars they had paid me for it. This was the last straw as far as father was concerned. I had now been with the Bowring firm for one and one-half years. Father then took me from the Bowring office and telegraphed Mr. Hayward to send me home on the *Portia*.

This ship (S.S. *Portia*) was then under the command of Captain Thomas Fitzpatrick, father of my wife to be. I had known Captain Fitzpatrick well -- had made his acquaintance during my period with the Bowring corporation and respected him highly. Captain Fitz-patrick was master of the S.S. *Algerine* when Bowring's first obtained the government coastal contract to operate a steamship service on the south west coast until such time as the *Portia* was delivered in St. John's. It was one of the mysteries of the sea, a feat of great bravery and seamanship, that the old *Algerine* ever survived. During one of her regular trips in the autumn of 1904, the *Algerine* ran into a hurricane and was driven off to sea, was missing for some twelve days, was given up as lost by everyone except Mrs. Fitzpatrick, who refused to believe that her husband would not return. Finally, after taking a thorough drubbing from the gale , after her hold and engine room had been flooded with water because of sprung leaks and other defects, this former old British gunboat turned up in Trepassey and eventually came to St. John's under her own steam. the story goes that Mr. Edgar Bowring, who was on the north side wharf to meet the ship on her return to St. John's, called out to Captain Fitzpatrick, "How are you feeling Captain?" Captain Fitzpatrick is said to have replied in this very modest tone: "Very well, Mr. Bowring, thank you." This is just another of those stories of the sea, a story which shows the courage and seamanship of our sturdy Newfoundland sailors. Another story is told of the at-titudes of the crew during these twelve days. Some of the more religious, feeling that death by drowning would soon overtake them, felt that they should all kneel down and pray, asking Almighty God to have mercy on them, by the recitation of the Holy Rosary. The mate, George O'Reilly of Placentia, is quoted as having said to them that they all must continue their work of trying to keep the ship from sinking. In fact he told them: "This is no time to curry favour with the Lord."

Chapter 3

I Return To Cape Broyle

The *Portia* backed off from Bowring's north side wharf on a cold Wednesday morning in November, 1907. The time was 10 a.m. She was bound on her regular round trip along the Southern Shore and the south west coast. I was one of the passengers on that ship headed for Cape Broyle, her first port-of-call on her outward passage. The wind was blowing a strong breeze down from the south west but the water was smooth. I walked the deck of that coastal boat in utter terror. I had more fear in my heart than at any time I later experienced in various battles in which I took part during the First World War in both France and Belgium. I could visualize what was coming to me when I arrived at Cape Broyle. We passed by Witless Bay, outside Green Island and Gull Island, and I could just make out faintly my grandmother's house, where I was reared as a youth up to ten years of age. I believe if the ship had called at Witless Bay, that I would have disembarked and stayed there. I would have been safe from all harm under the loving protection of that charming old Grandmother Mullowney. About 2 p.m. we arrived at Cape Broyle after four hours of steaming. The ship anchored about two hundred yards off the head of the Cashin wharf. There was not sufficient depth of water there to haul alongside and at that time there was no public wharf at Cape Broyle. We landed at the Cashin wharf in the mail boat. I proceeded to the house, our home. Mother received me kindly. We had supper about 6 p.m. My sister Mary and brother Martin, were then very young and were at home. Not a word was spoken at supper time. The cold silence gave me the creeps. Mother showed me to my room at the head of the stairs and I retired to bed about 9 p.m.

The morning following my return to Cape Broyle, I was given a suit of overalls and ordered to go over to the barn and clean the horse harness. I started in on this, my first job after my return from Bowring's office. About 10 a.m., father came around to the barn and came in to the compartment where I was doing the cleaning. He immediately proceeded to beat me up. He pounded me unmercifully and left me a heap of youthful wreckage, bleeding profusely. My premonition of the previous day was now a reality. I never raised my hand in self-defence. After he had departed following the vicious physical attack he had made upon me and after I had cleaned the scars from my bleeding nose and mouth, I began to think to myself what should I do. I made up my mind there and then, that as soon as I reached the age of twenty-one I would get out of Cape Broyle as well as Newfoundland as soon as I possibly could and I made up my mind to plan accordingly. During the remainder of the autumn months right up until Christmas, we were busy loading boats with dry fish and getting it away to St. John's. I was put to work at varied jobs, such as carrying the fish barrow and stowing dry fish in the holds of boats. No easy job for Peter any more while he stayed at Cape Broyle. Fortunately, I was in good health and my physical condition was improving all the time with lots of hard and heavy work. I did not have the privilege of working in the shop or of doing any office work. I was never in bed after six in the morning and everyone in the Cashin home was compelled to retire for the night not later than 10 p.m. I was very rarely out of that little bed after 9:30 p.m.

Personally, I did not consider I had committed any great crimes and in my own mind felt that I was being ill-treated by my father. I knew of his physical qualities and tried to avoid conflict in that respect as best I could. Christmas of 1907 was not a happy one for me in any way, shape or form. We had plenty to eat, I had good clothes to wear on Sundays, but no pay of any kind was given me. I had to depend entirely on the kindness of my mother for my smokes, and but for her generosity in that respect would have had to abandon this enjoyable habit. Mother made arrangements for me to go to another home each evening for a couple of hours to enjoy a smoke of the pipe. She provided both the pipe and tobacco and, in addition, I was able to scrounge the occasional cigarette from visitors or off the coastal boat when she came to Cape Broyle every two weeks. I do not believe I witnessed a smile from my father for the first three months after I had returned to Cape Broyle.

After Christmas that year there were many things to be done. Wood fuel had to be procured. We hired gangs of men to go into the woods to cut that wood and haul it to the head of Cape Broyle Pond. I accompanied these men, cut wood with them, cooked and ate with them. Then we had to haul the wood over the ice and I helped to load it on slides and drove a horse. When the ponds became frozen to a thickness of around eight inches of ice, we had to get to work and procure our ice for the purpose of supplying the Nova Scotia vessels when the months of June, July and August came around. All the horses and slides in the harbour were hired, special men were engaged to cut the ice with special saws. The ice was hauled a distance of nearly two miles. Another gang of specially selected and experienced men were engaged in stowing that ice in our two ice houses. This particular job was always under the supervision of Richard O'Brien ("Thumpy Dick") who was an expert at doing this kind of work. Getting in the ice was really a hectic week or more of real strenuous work. We always started long before daylight and worked until after dark. I had a couple of jobs at this particular work. I was ordered by father to tally the number of pieces of ice hauled by each horse and slide, whilst in addition I was compelled to work in the ice house stowing the ice when no loads of ice were around to tally. There was never an idle moment. No loafing on these jobs. No labour delegate to protest the slave-driving of men and horses. Nevertheless, I enjoyed the work both in the woods and at the ice house . It was a pleasure to be working alongside such fine characters of men and to observe the seriousness with which they carried out their respective jobs. It gave me a certain amount of freedom and relaxation. At night time I was permitted, through the good influence of my mother, to go over to Carrie Best's house for my usual smoke of the pipe. I enjoyed talking with dear old Carrie and her husband, John. Also, an old gentleman named Tom Johnson was a frequent visitor there and we were generally able to persuade Tom to sing his favourite song, called "Mother McCarthy's Daughter." Carrie Best was a Mullowney from Witless Bay, a first cousin of mother's as well as a loyal and faithful friend. She had been a school teacher for years before she married and in 1909 became postmistress at Cape Broyle. Carrie was always kind to me. She understood my little deficiences or faults, and I appreciated that kindness and human understanding on her part more than I can ever express in words.

During all the latter part of the winter, 1908, and the early spring, father was generally in St. John's attending the sessions of the House of Assembly. He was enthusiastically engaged in completing the foundation of the new political party which would have as its leader, during the 1908 autumn election, Sir Edward Morris. Morris had broken from the Bond government during the summer of 1907, using as an excuse for that break the policy of advocating a minimum wage for labour at government work of $1.25 per day of ten hours. The regular pay had previously been not more than 80¢ or $1.00 per day. When the legislature convened in the late winter of 1907, Morris took an Independent seat. He was not particularly active as an Independent member. He was kept busy working behind the scenes organizing a party for the general election which was to take place in the autumn of 1908. Father was the aggressor in all cases and the records of the House at that time show him in continuous conflict with several members of the Bond government. He generally made an effort, if at all possible, to come home to Cape Broyle for the weekends, driving over the road by horse and sleigh or coming by coastal boat. He was working like a Trojan to achieve his political ambitions, which, after Morris had left the Liberal Party, became even more strongly embedded in his system than ever.

We received the St. John's newspapers twice weekly and I read and reread all matter pertaining to the debates in the House of Assembly. P.T. McGrath, later Sir Patrick, who had been clerk of the House of Assembly as well as editor of the then *Evening Herald,* supporting Bond, had by this time followed Morris. McGrath organized a new daily newspaper called the *Chronicle,* the columns of which were particularly devoted to the denunciation of Bond and the advocacy of Morris as the next prime minister of Newfoundland. McGrath, although an invalid, was undoubtedly the most aggressive political writer Newfoundland has ever produced. In fact I am more or less confident that McGrath was the author of the 1908 manifesto of the "People's Party."

After the ice had been cleared away around the middle of February, 1908, father sent me all over the district of Ferryland soliciting subscriptions for this new political paper called the *Evening Chronicle.* I started in the southern end of the district and for the next several weeks visited every home from Cappahayden to Bay Bulls. I became acquainted with nearly all the people. I talked with them in their homes and, in my own youthful way, preached the Morris doctrine (I was just barely eighteen years old). At night time, in addition to soliciting subscriptions to this new political journal, I took part in any social events that might be taking place. I played the old time game of cards with many of the older people and became familiar with their habits and customs. This was, consequently, a great asset to me when I became a candidate for Ferryland in the general election held in the spring of 1923. Nearly all the Cashin supporters who had the money subscribed to this new paper for a period of from six to twelve months. The cost of an annual subscription was barely two dollars.

Then the spring of 1908 eventually came around. We were kept busy getting ready for the fishery. We had a couple of cod-traps operating on our own premises. The Cashin enterprise was supplying fishermen from Renews all along the shore as far as Tors Cove. A trap crew came into service around the middle of May. They were hired, or as we called it in those days, "shipped," for a period of two months or until August the 5th, or

10th. Their remuneration at the most was fifty dollars and found, which means food. In addition they were to receive a bonus of four dollars for every hundred quintals of fish caught. I had to do my share of this work. At times, I was a member of that trap crew, then skippered by old Jimmy O'Brien, "Suzie," as we called him. I helped to set out the moorings of the trap in Tar Cove. There was no such thing as motor engines at that time. We had to row when there was no wind or an unfavourable wind to sail. In the early morning, and I mean early (3 a.m.), we backed off from our wharf and rowed more than three miles to the trap berth. We generally had to row back, as the prevailing winds at that time of year were westerly. I rowed the bow oar of that old trap skiff on several occasions and before long was able to pull an eighteen foot spruce oar with the best of them. Our voyage that particular season in the traps was anything but successful. The Tar Cove berth which had given father such wonderful voyages in years gone by had now fallen down on its job. So M.P. Cashin decided to give up trapping codfish on his own premises in the future. He gave the traps to other fishermen to work out as best they could.

The latter part of June the Nova Scotia vessels fishing on the Grand Banks began coming in to Cape Broyle, Calvert and Aquaforte every week or ten days for the purpose of procuring fresh bait, ice and other essential supplies. We (the Cashin firm) did a great portion of this business. Fishermen with their own caplin seines generally hauled the caplin bait and it was our business to sell them the necessary ice. Later in the season these vessels bought squid baiting, paying at that time a price of around twenty cents for every hundred squid. In addition we purchased their common cod oil and old blubber. This blubber we landed by means of an old trap skiff. We emptied the blubber from the vessel's blubber butts into our own puncheons and then returned the empty butts to the vessels. The oil we extracted from this blubber sometimes paid off better than other times, as the Nova Scotia fishermen were expert in getting all the oil they could out of the rotting of the fish livers before selling the blubber.

Sometimes we drew a blank in this blubber business. It was then that father went to town on me. To me was delegated the responsibility of determining what the butts of blubber were worth and I made the necessary agreements with the captains of the vessels.

We had a special crew of men to handle this blubber and oil business. Sometimes our trap crew, when they procured no fish, would help out in the work, but generally it was left to three of us to do this job. My readers can be assured that it was a far dirtier job than making out bills or invoices in Bowring's office. I was fitted out with a suit of oil clothes, a pair of what we called in those days three-quarter leather boots, which were locally manufactured, and other working clothing appropriate for the job. After a couple of weeks at this work I felt in great physical shape. There were days during the month of July when we rowed a dory, two of us, at least ten miles, chasing Nova Scotia fishing vessels for business. I was in bed every night not later than nine o'clock. It was part of my duty to call the trap crew in the morning and I had to have them out of their bunks not later than 3 a.m. I had an alarm clock to wake me and was generally down on the road around 2:30 a.m. The men took their meals each day in what we called the back kitchen, but when the trap crew were leaving to haul the traps at such an early hour in the morning, there was a special box of food prepared for them the night before. We had four servant girls in those days. They were never in bed during the summer months after 5 a.m. and the two or three we had during the winter months were always on the job not later than 6 a.m. These fine young women were specially trained by my mother. I venture the opinion that it would be impossible to get people to work in that manner today.

Our land crew was also a specially selected body of men and a couple of young boys about my own age to handle the blubber, cod oil and ice for the Nova Scotia fishing vessels. We had a weird old gentleman in charge of the blubber and oil business. His name was Mr. Larry O'Neill. Mr. Larry, as we familiarly called him, was born in St. John's and came to Cape Broyle with my Grandfather Cashin years before father ever came into business. Skipper Larry was really an expert in the handling of these two products of the codfishery. Three of us young fellows at that time brought the blubber butts from the fishing vessels in an old dilapidated trap skiff, which we now called a blubber skiff. These three were myself, Stephen Carew, who died in the United States, and my old and good friend Jack Harvey. The three of us were tough young men. We had to be tough and strong to handle this particular job of getting the blubber butts loaded on the old leaky skiff, rowed ashore to our wharf, hoisted onto the wharf, emptied into our own puncheons and then the empty butts rowed back again to the vessels. That old skiff could take four of these butts in each load and we often made as high as eight trips daily to and from these Nova Scotia vessels.

Another of our scheduled jobs was to give ice to the banking vessels to ice down their caplin or squid baiting. This was also tough and sometimes difficult work. The ice was sold by the dory load and it was not uncommon for these Nova Scotia dorymen (Dutchmen as we called them) to try and overload their boats or to take more than a reasonable dory load. A dory can carry about one and a half tons of ice if it is properly stowed in the boat. Each vessel bought at least four dory loads and in those days the price was somewhere around five dollars per dory load. After they loaded this ice into the dories, they rowed it off to the vessels in the harbour, hoisted it aboard and the crew of the fishing craft began crushing it and icing down their bait. I have experienced in those times the handling of from fifty to one hundred dory loads of ice per day, which were thrown out of the ice house by myself, Jack Harvey and Stephen Carew.

After the 1905 legislation prohibiting the American fishing vessels coming into our harbours for bait and ice, that business was finished. However, the occasional American vessel would take a chance on coming to Cape Broyle for bait and we would give him his supplies during the night. I definitely remember two such incidents which occurred during the summer of 1908. In those days it was not considered a crime to do these things or to smuggle rum, tobacco or sugar from the French islands of St. Pierre and Miquelon. The only crime was in being caught. I played my part in a few of these smuggling ventures and we were fortunate in not having the representatives of the law catching up with us. When the American fishing vessels were coming into our harbours for bait, ice and other supplies, it was not unusual to have people take advantage of this opportunity of purchasing oil clothes, rubber boots, etc. This was very infrequent after the passing of the Foreign Fishing Vessels Act in 1905, but prior to that time it was almost a business to itself.

Again I must refer to that grand old gentleman, Larry O'Neill. He was loyal to the Cashin family and was constantly in conflict with the Nova Scotia vessel masters over the quality of their blubber butts. Mr. Larry also assisted my mother in the gauging of the numerous casks of cod oil purchased from these vessels when father was away. In fact, I go so far as to state that mother could do that job even better than my father. Larry O'Neill was really a landmark on the Cashin premises. He never missed a Sunday morning coming down to the house before Mass to get his usual good "horn of rum." He wore three-quarter leather boots all the time and on Sundays they were shined better than any one can have their shoes shined today by any professional shoeshiner on the mainland. He was clean and tidy on Sundays. One would hardly think it was the same man who was handling blubber the previous week.

In the summer time, Mother generally had a few lady visitors from St. John's for a holiday or just a few days visit. She never failed to bring them down on the wharf and introduce them to Mr. Larry O'Neill. He was the type of man who took a great delight in disgusting some of these St. John's ladies. I remember distinctly on one occasion, three such persons were brought down on the wharf by Mother to be introduced to Skipper Larry. He was busy at the time putting blubber into specially made brin bags to be pressed out for any oil that might remain in the rotten livers. He always filled these bags with his hands. He always chewed tobacco. In fact he very rarely spat out the juice. He nearly always swallowed it. When Mother introduced these three ladies to Skipper Larry, he paid little or no attention to them. He continued at his job, handling the blubber with his hands and chewing his tobacco, the juice of which was streaming down his old grey whiskers. This action on his part was most distasteful to these three St. John's ladies. At first it almost made them sick to their stomachs. To round off the official introduction, Mr. Larry took a handful of the old rotten blubber out of one of the puncheons and began eating it. That action on his part rung down the curtain on this official introduction to this veteran oil man, who had been so long with and loyal to the Cashin family. Larry was one of that type who could tell off my father in no uncertain manner and get away with it. He knew more about the production of cod oil in every way than any other man I have ever known. In truth, he was a great asset to the Cashin business at Cape Broyle.

During the latter part of August or the early part of September, 1908, which was my first summer at Cape Broyle, the fishermen whom we had supplied for the prosecution of the codfishery had begun to bring in their early fish. The expression used in these outports at that time: "they were putting off their fish." This meant a continuation of additional work for three or four of us who were employed for the entire season. The trap crew had been paid off and they had now gone fishing handline, either in boats of their own or in boats with other handline fishermen. Sometimes we had to hire extra help when it became too busy for three or four of us to handle. In addition to young boys whom we engaged for handling fish we also had two or three women working stowing fish in stores and spreading it on the flakes. We had our own trap fish to cure. To do this we had to wash it out in the stage. Then it would lay in bulk for a day or two and we would carry or wheel it onto the flakes in wheelbarrows. This was what is commonly called "waterhorse." There was no such thing as official weather forecasting as we have today. We had to rely on our own judgment as to whether or not it would be a good day for the curing of shore fish.

My experience tells me that some of these old-time fishermen were better judges, or at least as good, as our modern meteorological experts. The latter are not infrequently all astray in their forecasts.

When the codfish was properly stored and piled in bulk in our two stores, known at that time as the "long store" and the "short store," the next thing was the shipping and selling of that commodity. We never entered into the export fish business from Cape Broyle. Father always looked after the sale of our codfish and was generally able to obtain special prices from Bowring's, to whom we nearly always shipped our fish. To do this we had to load it in boats carrying from four to five hundred quintals (112 lbs. to a quintal). We needed fine weather to load these little craft and it generally took a full fine day for five or six of us to load the boat, the crew stowing the fish in the hold. At that time the freight per quintal from Cape Broyle to St. John's was about ten cents. We operated one of these boats ourselves, but she was not sufficient to handle all our collection, so other coasters had to be chartered or hired. We nearly always had the old *Mary Ellen,* owned and skippered by Pierre Ronayne of Tors Cove, whom I have already referred to in the early part of this book. We had the *Norah,* owned and skippered by Martin Chidley of Cape Broyle. We had a boat operated by Tim Nagle of Tors Cove and the *May Queen*, owned and skippered by Andy Aspell of Admirals Cove, Cape Broyle. Father was nearly always in St. John's when these boats arrived, to see that they received quick dispatch. Generally they were given a return freight of all kinds of goods for the shop and retail stores. We were informed by telegram when they would leave St. John's and were always ready to start unloading immediately they tied up at the wharf at Cape Broyle.

During the latter part of the summer of 1908, I learned how to cull out the various qualities of fish. If father was at home, he did the weighing and on numerous occasions when he was away, mother did that job just as efficiently if not better. I can assure my readers that mother always saw to it that she received her good weight. I doubt if we ever turned out a shortage. In addition to culling the fish on several occasions, I also was one of the regular barrowmen carrying the fish to the stores or on board the boats for shipment to St. John's. On real fine days, with a fresh breeze of westerly or north-west wind, it was part of my job to see that the windows and doors of the fish stores were open, so that the bulked fish would receive the benefit of the cool dry air created by such winds.

Then, in the autumn of 1908, the general election took place. Father was a candidate for the People's Party under the leadership of Sir Edward Morris. His colleague was the late Mr. Philip Coady Moore, a well-known citizen of St. John's, whose mother came from Fermeuse and who was a distant relative of my father. Mr. W.J. Ellis, together with Mr. Robert Moore, master cooper, were the opposing candidates under the leadership of Sir Robert Bond. As I previously related, Mr. Ellis was a highly respected gentleman and had been instrumental in many ways for having certain public works carried out in the district of Ferryland. As an example, I would refer to the dredging of Renews Harbour. Renews is one of the best locations on the southern shore for fishing. The story goes that, when one of the old Goodridge family was dying, his last words were to "keep salt in Renews." The firm of Goodridge and Sons had several branches along the Southern Shore and old man Goodridge evidently looked upon Renews as a most profitable fishing ground. The harbour is exposed to the sea and the water is very shallow. After father had resigned from Bond's party in 1905, Mr. Ellis was responsible for the expenditure of all government money in Ferryland District. He took good care of this political advantage and saw to it that the harbour of Renews was dredged. In fact, that harbour is so exposed to the sea that it is almost essential to have a channel dredged there every couple of years. Whilst father was elected at the head of the poll for the fifth consecutive time, Ellis was also elected, beating father's running mate, Phil Moore, by just a little over fifty votes. I would judge from my knowledge of that election that the split vote in Renews elected Mr. Ellis. When the final returns from all the

Newfoundland constituencies were completed, they showed that both parties had eighteen members.

When Morris began the organization of his People's Party in the summer of 1908, he had many difficult political obstacles to overcome. One of the principal of these problems was the handling of A.B. Morine. Morine had been leader of the opposition in the House of Assembly. The name Morine was and always remained a bugaboo in Newfoundland politics. How was Morris going to deal with such a situation? By some unknown method or other, Morris was able to arrange that Morine would get out of Newfoundland, and the story goes that the Reids, whose solicitor Morine had been for many years, were able to make a deal with Morine to retire to Canada for a period of ten years at an annual salary from the Reid Company of ten thousand dollars. This clever political move on the part of Sir Edward Morris took Morine out of political life and removed a burden from the People's Party.

As a result of this tie election great excitement prevailed all over the island. Everyone wondered what would happen when the legislature convened during the winter of 1909. In the meantime efforts were being made by agents of both the Bond party and the Morris party to induce members to leave one side or the other. Political promises were the order of the day. In one particular case, a representative of the Bond party made an effort to sell himself to the Morris party. He tried to arrange a meeting with the leader of the People's Party, Sir Edward Morris. This individual member of the Bond party went so far as to dress himself up in women's clothing, so as not to be recognized. Morris refused to meet him. In another instance one of the members of the Bond party had sold himself to the Morris party and had actually received a sum of money for his betrayal. His mother forced him to return the money and remain with Bond. Finally, the House of Assembly opened in the early part of 1909. Neither side could elect a Speaker. Sir Robert Bond then asked the Governor, who at that time was Sir William McGregor, for a dissolution of the House, so that he could go to the country for another election.

The Governor refused Bond's request. He then called upon Sir Edward Morris, who undertook to form a government. Morris formed a new government and by some political manipulation was able to have His Excellency the Governor grant him a dissolution and another general election took place in the spring of 1909.

Again, father and Phil Moore contested the constituency of Ferryland on behalf of the Morris party. M.P. Cashin had now achieved one of his ambitions, a position which he had set himself to attain when he left the Bond party in 1905. He was now Minister of Finance and Customs in the Morris government, which carried with it a seat in the cabinet. Their two opponents in this spring election were Mr. George Power, a cooper from St. John's, and Mr. M.E. Condon of Cape Broyle, who had been nominated as an Independent candidate on several previous elections. Mr. Ellis, the Bond candidate in the 1908 election, had chosen to oppose Sir Edward Morris in the district of St. John's West. He was defeated. Father was elected for the sixth time in his native district at the head of the poll and his colleague, Mr. Phil Moore, was also elected by a substantial majority. In addition, the Morris government had succeeded in winning several constituencies which it had lost in the autumn election of 1908. For instance, Placentia, which had returned three Bond men in 1908, now returned three Morris men. Even "the great Jackman" was defeated. Carbonear had turned over from Liberal to the People's Party. Trinity, which had given Bond three seats in 1908, also turned over and gave Morris another three men. The final results of that spring election of 1909, necessitated by the tie election of 1908, gave Morris twenty-six members against ten for Bond. The People's Party was now strongly entrenched in office. It was in a position to carry out its policy of the extension of the railway system, or what they called it at that time, the building of branch railways to Bonavista, Trepassey and Heart's Content, as well as the extension of the Carbonear branch down to Bay-de-Verde.

It cannot be overlooked that the success of the People's Party under the leadership of Sir Edward

Morris was in a great measure due to the political astuteness and strategy of this phenomenal figure, E.P. Morris. Edward Patrick Morris came into public life in Newfoundland in 1885. He had just been admitted to the Bar and was barely twenty six years old. He contested the great district of St. John's West and ten consecutive times was elected for that constituency. There are so many stories told about the political moves and tactics of Morris during his various political contests that it would be a book all to itself if I began relating them. However, there is one particular episode which I feel worth relating, as, to me at any rate, it is both amusing and serves to portray the knowledge he had of the Newfoundland temperament. In one particular election, one of many of his political henchmen reported to Sir Edward one morning that a certain individual in the St. John's West constituency was bitterly opposed to him. Morris' reply was that he would go up and see that individual that same evening. His henchman begged him not to go, as he felt that he would be insulted, if not actually assaulted. However, Morris went to the house of this potential opponent the same evening. It happened that the man's wife conducted a small shop, selling lemonade, candies, etc. When Sir Edward entered the shop, the lady was astounded. Morris asked her for a bottle of lemonade. Whilst he was drinking the lemonade, he heard music coming from an organ located in the back room, just behind the little shop. He asked the lady: "Who is playing that organ?" She replied that it was her little girl. "May I come in and listen to her," asked Sir Edward? The lady agreed, and so Sir Edward went behind, sat down and listened to this innocent youngster play several pieces of simple music in the usual childish fashion. Morris was waiting for the man of the house, who he had been told was so bitterly opposed to him, to return. Finally the man came in and was practically dumbfounded when he saw Sir Edward sitting in the old rocking chair in the small sitting room. Sir Edward immediately rose from the seat, said good night to the man and his wife, further adding that he had never heard such music in all his life and suggesting that when he was elected Prime

Minister of Newfoundland, he would see to it that this particular young girl would be sent to the Conservatoire of Music in Paris to complete her musical education. He walked out without saying another word. The following day the voters in the neighbourhood were surprised to find this same individual voter out working his head off for Morris. Morris never missed going to funerals in his district of St. John's West. He often showed up to as many as two or three of these and parades the same afternoon. He wanted the people to see that he had not forgotten them. He always carried an umbrella - rain or shine. In this respect he resembled Neville Chamberlain, a former Prime Minister of Great Britain. There was one difference; Morris never "missed the bus" politically.

During the 1908-09 election campaigns Morris visited every important section of the island. He was a Roman Catholic, and hundreds of people thought he could never be elected as Prime Minister. However, Sir Edward was shrewd enough politically to gather around him men of the calibre of Donald Morrison and young Richard A. Squires, the latter working in his office at the study of law. Despite the fact that he was a Roman Catholic, and further, despite the fact that the late Archibishop Howley was most outspoken against him, he finally achieved his ambition by being elected Prime Minister on May the 8th, 1909. He played the game of politics on that day, because May the 8th was his fiftieth birthday and Morris was not slow in taking advantage of even this small incident. He also had a behind-the-scenes adviser in the person of P.T. McGrath, who, whilst he was generally unpopular because of his unscrupulous and fearless writings, had the keenest of political judgment, in addition to which he had the case history of every politician of the time. In my opinion Morris was our greatest and most cagey politician. He had the happy knack of being capable of getting around him in his party other politicians, such as Cashin, Crosbie, Squires and Morrison, who were also efficient in the art of vote-getting. Morris was our only Newfoundlander, who came from the ranks of the people, who made a profession of politics, who had virtually no financial means, but who finally ended up by being elevated to the peerage and appointed to a seat in Britain's House of Lords. He, too, had his political faults and later in these memoirs will be related some of his misdeeds.

I cannot pass over some incidents which occurred during the elections of 1908-09 without commenting on the tactics which were used, particularly in the district of Ferryland, to defeat the Morris candidates. There was no question but that the great majority of the Roman Catholic clergy openly advocated the Liberal Party and in some cases strongly denounced the representatives of the People's Party. The late Archbishop Howley was an outstanding and active supporter of the Liberal Party under the leadership of Sir Robert Bond. The majority of the Roman Catholic clergy located in the various parishes of Ferryland constituency were, as a result of the Archbishop's prejudice against Morris, strongly opposed to both my father and his colleague. In two particular incidents, they were openly canvassing for the Bond representatives. The same tactics applied in other Catholic constituencies in the archdiocese of St. John's. The historic district of Ferryland was at that time and still is, practically all comprised of Roman Catholic people. In Witless Bay and in Tors Cove, the clergy were particularly hostile to father and his colleague. They used every effort possible to induce the people to vote for the Bond representatives. In spite of this strong hostility on the part of these good priests, Cashin and Moore were elected by safe majorities and father headed the poll for the sixth time.

I will never forget the night of polling day, May 1909. In those days the ballot boxes were brought to Ferryland by horse and carriage to be counted. There was no other means of transportation. Immediately the polls closed the ballot boxes were sealed and the necessary papers filled out by the various deputy returning officers and polling clerks, then one messenger picked up the boxes from the Goulds and at each booth room from there to Ferryland. Another messenger collected the boxes at Cappahayden and from there along the shore until he reached Ferryland. There would be a driver in addition to the messenger. When the boxes arrived at Ferryland they would be checked by the returning officer before being counted.

In this election (1909), my uncle, Louis Mullowney of Witless Bay was the driver from the Goulds to Ferryland. The messenger was Alphonsus Mullowney. Uncle Louis had a very fast horse. When he hauled out on the main road after leaving the Goulds, he noticed that he was being followed, and he recognized the individual who was following him. He was Patrick Tobin of Witless Bay, accompanied by James Burke of the same place, both strong political opponents of my father. It appears that during the course of a political meeting which my father was addressing in the open air at Witless Bay, Tobin had hidden himself under a fish flake, continually heckling and using insulting language. Father ascertained that the heckler in question was Tobin. When Uncle Louis arrived at Tors Cove on his way to Ferryland, he telegraphed my father that he was being followed by Tobin and asked him if he had any suggestions to make. Father replied immediately to Uncle Louis, telling him that when he arrived at Cape Broyle he should drive right over into our back yard. He figured that Tobin would follow Uncle Louis and he figured right. Prior to the arrival of the two horses and carriages, Cashin sent Jack Harvey, who was then working with us, for the local police officer. At that time the police officer in question was Constable Thomas Lynch, who was highly respected in the community. He told Lynch that he wanted him to look after the ballot boxes when they arrived, as my uncle would be staying at Cape Broyle for a cup of tea. We knew that it would take an hour or a little more for these two horses to come from Tors Cove. Shortly before the expiration of an hour, father ordered me to light the lantern. It was late at night and there was no electric light along the shore at that time. Finally we heard the horses come down over the hill, and eventually both of them arrived in our back yard. I accompanied father out into the yard with the lantern, so that he could see who the people were. The first arrival was my uncle with the official messenger. Then Tobin and his friend Burke arrived. Father asked Uncle Louis what was all this about, and he replied that Pat Tobin and Jimmy Burke had been following him all night. At once Father went to Tobin's carriage. I held the lantern so that he could see both Tobin and Burke. Immediately he asked them what they were doing on his property, whilst at the same time he reached up and grabbed Tobin by the collar, pulled him out of the carriage and gave him an awful beating. He hit Tobin several times, knocking down a new fence which was being erected. Burke, who was just a little man, started crying and bawling, saying, "Oh, Mr. Cashin, do not do this." Then father took hold of Burke, hit him a few times, and finally threw him at Tobin. Following this, he threw both Tobin and Burke back into their carriage and told them in no uncertain language to get out of his yard. They proceeded to Ferryland where the district magistrate, at that time Dr. Freebairn, was located. They wanted to take action against father for assault. I understand that Dr. Freebairn told them that they had no legal case, as they had trespassed on Cashin's property. These two individuals (Tobin and Burke) stayed in Ferryland all night. The following day, they procured the protection of Constable Cleary of Ferryland to take them through Cape Broyle. They were afraid to drive through the settlement on their own in case Cashin would again attack them. Tobin certainly suffered for the personal insults he had thrown at father at that particular public meeting in Witless Bay. On the other hand, it was just another example of the violent temper with which my respected father was unfortunately afflicted. He was at that time a minister of the Crown, and in my personal view, now that I have become, as it were, indoctrinated in the hurly burly of political life, I consider that father would have treated poor Tobin and Burke with greater effect, if he had completely ignored them. It certainly would have been more dignified on his part.

Even though I did not have a vote during the elections of 1908-09, I learned considerable about the manner in which election campaigning had been carried out in the district. I had come to know practically every individual person in the district. I had listened to the people talking about the coming election of 1908. I continually read the daily papers which were supporting each party. I had acted as general agent in booth rooms for my father and his colleague. I am sure that at that time I could tell how every man voted in the settlement of Cape Broyle. These two elections were really the groundwork of my political education and served me well some fifteen years later, when I became a candidate in that good old district of Ferryland.

I was particularly impressed, from a political point of view, with the manner in which the candidates on both sides conducted their campaigns in 1908-09. I was specially impressed during the 1908 autumn campaign with the joint meetings held by representatives of the two parties. My father knew that Mr. Ellis was strong in the district, but he also figured that, if he could arrange joint meetings, he would be able to out-talk Mr. Ellis. Because the latter, whilst he was a thoroughly honourable man in every respect, was not what one would call a good debater on public matters. Father's judgment in this respect was again correct. I clearly remember the joint meeting they held in the open air at Cape Broyle. The four candidates spoke from the gallery of what we called "the old shop." Mr. Ellis and his colleague, Mr. Robert Moore, were no match in debate for M.P. Cashin. There was no personal abuse. Each representative or candidate put his case for his party before the people fairly and squarely. In the final analysis, as always, the people were the judges. In the spring election of 1909, it was conceded by everyone that Cashin would bring his colleague, Phil Moore, through with himself, and the result was that good old Ferryland gave another man to the Morris People's Party.

Now that the new government under Sir Edward Morris was definitely confirmed in office, and father confirmed in his post as Minister of Finance and Customs, he spent the greater portion of his time in St. John's. Sometimes he drove over the road to spend Saturday and Sunday at Cape Broyle to see for himself how business generally was progressing . Mother was the driving force behind the entire commercial enterprise.

The previous year of 1908, as I have already related, I worked at all kinds of labour in connection with the handling of codfish, blubber and cod oil as well as chasing the Nova Scotia vessels for business. I had nothing whatever to do with the shop, store or office in 1908. However, in 1909, I was, should I say, given some promotion. I had to take care of the fishermen's accounts. I weighed and culled codfish in addition to doing plenty of ordinary labouring work. We were now supplying fishermen for the prosecution of the codfishery from Renews to Tors Cove. Also, I was sent by father to buy fish at Aquaforte. I had to cull and weigh this fish and supervise the proper loading of the product in boats. I had to be unusually careful that the various boat cargoes turned out their proper weights. Yes, I had to be more than careful to make certain that when the fish was reculled on arrival at St. John's that my selection or culling was correct. I was lucky in this respect. There were times in carrying out this fish buying job at Aquaforte, Ferryland, Calvert and Witless Bay when I lived aboard the boat with the crew. Other times, I drove home late at night from Aquaforte, Ferryland or Calvert. When at Witless Bay I always stayed with my sweet old Grandmother Mullowney. She treated me as she always did and continued to call me her boy, Peter.

I certainly was kept going during the summer of 1909. There were no idle moments. I had gained considerable experience in the handling of fish, and when father sent me out to buy fish or make bargains for the purchase of certain lots of fish, I was generally lucky in being able to turn out a profit. When home at Cape Broyle I weighed and culled the fish which the fishermen brought in. Naturally, sometimes I made a mistake. Who doesn't? When I made these occasional errors in judgment I came in for aggressive action from my father. Very little, if any, credit was ever given me for the things I might have done properly, or the success I made in buying codfish which would turn out a favourable profit. I was supposed to be PERFECT in every respect. In my fifty years of experience in all walks of life, in all kinds of jobs, jobs both in Newfoundland and the mainland of Canada, I have yet to find the individual, no matter what his capabilities might be, who did not make the occasional error.

I remember distinctly one error I made in the compilation of an account for a Nova Scotia vessel. It did not amount to more than ten dollars. As father usually came home for the weekend, he was checking these accounts and discovered this error of mine on Sunday morning, just after mass. Jack Harvey, to whom I have previously referred, was in the shop when father drew this mistake of mine to his attention. He became furious with me and again lost his temper. He took hold of an oak gauging rod which was behind the shop counter and made an attempt to strike me across the back with it. Fortunately for myself I was able to dodge the blow. Instead of hitting me with this particular instrument, he hit the counter with such force that the gauging rod was split in two parts. Maybe if the blow had struck me as poor father had intended, it would have maimed me for life and my deformity would have taught him a lesson for the future. My father was then forty-five years old and really in the prime of life.

Following this unfortunate incident, I became more determined than ever to get out of Cape Broyle at the first possible opportunity. That particular season was a very busy one indeed. We handled considerable fish from our local dealers on our Cape Broyle premises and, in addition, I purchased and shipped to St. John's several thousand quintals from Aquaforte, Ferryland and Witless Bay. In all, we must have handled upwards of ten thousand quintals of shore codfish that year. In a few cases we even bought salt-bulk fish from the Nova Scotia banking vessels and cured it ourselves on our flakes at Cape Broyle.

One Sunday afternoon in September of 1909, Sir Edgar Bowring came up as far as Cape Broyle in his motor car. It was a glorious day, the wind was westerly, the sun was shining brightly and, as usual, I had all the fish store doors and windows open, so that the cool air would circulate. I remember Sir Edgar coming in to what we called our long store that Sunday afternoon. He began looking at the fish and asking me questions about its general quality and enquiring how many quintals we had on hand. I gave him all the information he asked for. Then, suddenly, the thought struck me to ask him for a berth to the ice (the seal fishery) the coming spring in the *Florizel*. Bowring's had built this ship to run on the New York, Halifax and St. John's route during the summer months. She had been specially constructed so that she could contend with heavy ice. She had been in command of Captain Abraham Kean during the spring of 1909 and secured over thirty thousand seals. Mr. Bowring told me that he would do this for me, and asked me to write him about a month before the sealfishing voyage in 1910. I told my mother what I had done and later, when he came home to Cape Broyle for the next weekend, I told father. I had it in my mind to take up the sea as an avocation, to become a sailor and eventually try and work myself up to become a master of a ship. Neither father or mother objected to this at the time. I was highly elated at my prospects. We had a very successful season in 1909 and the prospects for 1910 looked very bright indeed.

The winter of 1910 came around with the necessity of getting wood fuel cut and hauled as well as ice cut and stored for the coming season. Then around the early part of February, I wrote Sir Edgar Bowring, reminding him of the promise he had given me the previous autumn regarding a berth to the sealfishery in the S.S. *Florizel*. Sir Edgar replied immediately, advising me to come along when the sealers would be signing on the various ships and telling me that I would be given the promised berth in the *Florizel*. Great preparations were now being made for my sealing venture. Mother, God bless her, prepared all kinds of essential clothing, had a special sailor's box made for me and also had the girls busy preparing all kinds of cakes and other food not available on such a voyage. I well remember the afternoon I left Cape Broyle by horse and slide to travel over the road to St. John's. Jack Harvey was with me to drive the horse. There was a lot of snow on the road and in certain places it was difficult to get along. We stopped at Witless Bay to have some food, give the horse a feed and rest before we left for the final leg of the journey to the city. My dear old Grandmother Mullowney was delighted with me. No doubt she felt that I would follow in Grandfather Mullowney's footsteps and eventually become master of a sealer. We arrived in St. John's around ten or eleven o'clock at night. I went to the old Balmoral Hotel opposite the general post office, which was operated by Mrs. McGrath. It was now March the 9th, and I had celebrated my twentieth birthday the day before leaving Cape Broyle. I had not been near St. John's since I left Bowring's office in November, 1907. The following day we signed on the ship's articles and that same evening father, with several other members of the government, left St. John's by train for Grand Falls, to attend the official opening of the first pulp and paper mill in Newfoundland. The day after signing on, we were kept busy getting our clothes aboard and selecting our living quarters, which were anything but comfortable. The sealers lived in the hold of the vessel, special bunks having been built up for sleeping quarters. Being a steel ship, she was anything but warm for comfortable rest. There were three other Southern Shore men members of the crew, namely, Bob Walsh of Fermeuse, Jack Brazil of Renews and Mike Kelly of Cape Broyle. These men had made several trips to the sealfishery. The four of us kept together and managed to be put in the same watch under a fine master-watchman by the name of Joseph Sturge. Peculiarly enough there was an old gentleman by the name of Roberts, who came from Brigus North, who was a wheelsman on the ship, and had been to the sealfishery with my Grandfather Mullowney in the old *Ranger,* away back in 1871. This was the last voyage Pierre Mullowney made to the frozen icefields.

We were scheduled to sail for the great sealing venture on the evening of March 12th. A clerk from Bowring's office began calling the roll at 4 p.m. There were some 203 men answered that roll call. We backed out from Harvey's wharf that evening with all flags flying. There were hundreds of people on the pier to see us off and bid us godspeed with a bumper trip. We headed north from St. John's and were abeam of Cape Bonavista early the next morning in loose ice. I did not sleep much that night as I was not accustomed to living in such cramped-up quarters. I had one consolation, and that was that my companions were men I knew well from the Southern Shore. Poor Bob Walsh was our guide in every respect. He was a most religious man and he was a noble character. He saw to it that we said our night prayers each night before we retired.

On the morning of March the 13th, it was discovered that we had a stowaway on board. In those days many young men tried to stow away to the sealfishery on the various sealing vessels. In this case, it transpired that our stowaway was a man from Quidi Vidi by the name of Hennebury. His avocation in life was that of what is termed nowadays a truckman. He had left his horse and cart in front of the old mechanics' hall on Water Street, imbibed a little too freely, then he came aboard to see a friend of his off to the sealing voyage. He slept that night on the fore hatch of the ship, and when he woke up the next morning he found himself on board the *Florizel* heading for the great sealing venture. He was cold and naturally he was shivering, but he was certainly a specimen of a hardy Newfoundlander. Hennebury knew some of the firemen and he ate and slept in their quarters, which were apart from the ordinary members of the sealing crew.

As this fine ship steamed North towards the vicinity of the Funk Islands we gradually ran into heavier ice and at times it became necessary to use powder to blow a channel for her to get free and continue on her course. She generally got stuck amidships. We carried, in addition to full bunkers of coal, an additional supply of what we called "Yankee slack" in the hold. During the night time, the crew of which I was a member took their turns in passing that coal from the hold into the bunkers. As we were working in heavy ice and the ship must consume at least 45 tons of coal fuel daily, it was necessary to keep the bunkers filled at all times. We used a certain type of basket to do this job and I can assure my readers it was anything but pleasant. For five days and nights we continued to break our way through this thick ice. The *Eagle,* another of Bowring's ships, was continuously in contact with our ship by wireless telegraphy, which by the way, was used for the first time that year at the sealfishery. It proved invaluable to the owners of both these ships as one was continuously in touch with the other. Captain Abraham Kean of the *Florizel* was the father of Captain Joe Kean of the *Eagle* and naturally one was doing his utmost to advise and help out the other. Within sight of our ship were the *Bellaventure, Bonaventure* and *Beothic,* all three steel ships, following more or less in our wake. We had been issued with our gaffs and hauling ropes and were all ready to take to the frozen pans immediately we would strike the seals.

Finally, on March the 17th (St. Patrick's Day), about ten or eleven o'clock in the morning we steamed right into what Captain Kean figured was the main body of seals. Captain Kean went forward on the forecastle head and shot the first old seal. Our position on the chart showed us somewhere in the vicinity of the Gray Islands. Following the shooting by Captain Kean of the old seals, all hands were ordered on the ice and killing began in earnest. We cleaned up this small patch in a short while and then all hands boarded the ship and after a few hours steaming struck the real "main patch." We all took to the ice again and this time we carried on with even more enthusiasm. I worked on the ice with the three Ferryland men who showed me how to kill and then skulp the seals. It was really a wonderful sight to see thousands, yes, scores of thousands, of these young seals all around you. Each watch went in different directions and before long the kill began in real earnest. Really, I felt sorry for these young seals. I was forced to say to myself that it was a cruel thing to kill them. The old-time sealers laughed at me. Very soon I was indoctrinated into the manner of killing, skulping and hauling to ice-pans these young seals. We killed these seals with what is called a gaff. A gaff is a wooden instrument to which is attached a steel hook to help you walking over slippery ice, and if necessity arises and a man should fall in the water, the gaff is used to pull him out. All one had to do to kill these young seal harps, was to hit them on the nose with the gaff, then turn them over and skin the fat and skin off them, leaving the carcass on the ice. Then we towed them with a special tow-rope to special spots or ice-pans, placing the ship's flag on such pan. They then could be picked up by the ship or, if not, towed again to the vessel. Again I say it was most pathetic to look at these young harps when you walked up to kill them. They would look up at you with actual tears in their eyes and it took me a few hours to be a real seal-killer. After the first day, I was trained in the art of killing and could haul on the tow rope as many seals as the average man aboard the ship. We were on the ice from daylight until dark. The first day was a dirty, foggy one and we could not see very far. We carried certain emergency food with us. This generally consisted of oatmeal, sugar and raisins all mixed together and carried in what is called a "ninny bag" attached to your belt.

The second morning we had to go over the side of the ship which was high out of the water, I felt frightfully stiff. I could barely lift one leg over the rail but somehow or other was able to climb down the ladder to the ice. I had not been accustomed to walking on slippery ice for any length of time and the soles of my sealskin boots were not properly "frosted." However, I managed to get on the ice and after an hour I had worked the stiffness out of my legs. From then onwards I was in great shape. No more stiffness. Despite the poor cooking and filthy work, I became accustomed to do everything a regular sealer should do. I never missed a day working on the ice at seals. At night time all the crew were kept busy hoisting aboard seals from the ice-pans as well as the usual passing of coal into the bunkers. I was generally engaged at night with a suit of oil clothes on me, in addition to my regular sealing outfit, at guiding the wire hoisting cable to the hold and signalling the winchmen. It was a dirty job but I enjoyed it. I much preferred it to the job of passing that dusty "Yankee slack coal."

That particular season (1910) we had, as I remember, some five passengers on board — people who went to the ice for the pleasure they could get out of it. Mr. Eric Bowring was one of the passengers. I am greatly indebted to Mr. Bowring for permitting me to use the diary which he kept of that one and only sealing venture of mine. From Mr. Bowring's diary, I was able to secure information with regards to certain incidents that occurred during that notable trip. In addition to Mr. Bowring, there were the late Honourable C.P. Ayre, Mr. Herbert Outerbridge, later president of the firm of Harvey & Co., Ltd., Mr. Herbert Winter and Mr. Harold Harvey. These fine men, who represented the cream of our mercantile firms at that time, certainly enjoyed their experiences and worked at the killing, hauling and general handling of seals. Mr. Bowring, according to his diary, was something like myself. He, too, felt it was an act of cruelty to kill these young seals. He, too, had sympathy for these little animals as they looked up at him from the ice with tears in their dark eyes. He admitted in his diary that he was not overanxious to either kill or skulp these seals. Nevertheless, Mr. Bowring, as I remember, was able to haul a tow of seals as good if not better than any man aboard that ship. He was young at the time and was a very strong man, was in good physical shape, being one of our outstanding athletes at that period. Mr. Bowring also made special reference to the cold quarters in which the crew were compelled to live. He referred generally to the very frosty weather and heavy sheet ice which the men had to contend with. On several days quite a number of the regular sealers were compelled to stay aboard ship as they had been stricken with colds and in some cases became ice-blind. I was fortunate in this respect. I felt in such good physical condition, that I could tackle any kind of job the other experienced men were able to perform.

The chief navigation officer aboard the ship was an old friend of mine from my early years at Bowring's. This was Captain J.R. Williams, who was master of the steel vessel *Margaret Murray* when first she came to Newfoundland. Any spare time I had, and that was little, was spent talking with Captain Williams in his room. I had asked him to give me a job that coming summer on the S.S. *Rosalind,* which was to run between St. John's, Halifax, New York and later on the St. John's to Montreal route. Captain Williams very kindly offered me a job as deck hand, as I was seriously considering going to sea and working for my master's certificate. I was destined never to be given this opportunity.

We continued working at the seals on the ice, killing and hauling, then loading. After about ten days Captain Kean decided to bear up for home. I believe that, because of the fact the *Florizel* had to take up the regular Red Cross route between St. John's, Halifax and New York around the first part of May, the captain had instructions to be back in port around the first of April. It would take at least a month to clean up the ship and put her in shape to handle passengers and general cargo after such a trip, as the prosecution of the sealfishery, naturally, would create a lot of dirt and filthy odour which would take considerable time to dispose of.

The 1910 season proved the value of the steel ships as compared to the old wooden sealers that had been formerly used to carry out this annual sealing adventure. It proved that the old wooden ships had not the steam power or the strength to contend with heavy ice. This particular season nearly all the old wooden ships failed to get paying trips. With the exception of the *Eagle, Algerine* and *Newfoundland* the wooden fleet drew practically a blank. The spring, generally, was a stormy one. It was unusually cold and there were days it was impossible to see any great distance because of low-lying fog. Men suffered, as I have related, from severe colds, and Mr. Bowring, in his diary, strongly advocated that necessary facilities be provided in future for the comfort of the crew. This was the year the old wooden sealer, *Iceland,* was crushed in the ice and had to be abandoned. Her crew of some 150 men were picked up by the *Eagle* and then transferred to our ship when we were homeward bound. We also were in a position to give the *Aurora,* another of Bowring's ships, some coal. She had run short and as she had not been so successful in getting into the main   patch as the *Florizel,* Captain Greene, an old friend of mine from the days I was junior clerk in the Bowring office, decided to stay out longer in order to try and pick up what old seals he could to make a paying trip. These two actions of taking on board the wrecked crew of the *Iceland* and the giving of coal to the *Aurora* were the last things we did before straightening out for home.

The day before our arrival at St. John's we had to contend with very heavy sheet ice and had great difficulty in getting through. Finally, on the morning of April 1st, we passed Cabot Island about 7 a.m. The entire crew were jubilant. All those on board were getting both themselves and part of the ship cleaned up for the glorious entry into the harbour of St. John's. We knew that we had an official tally of over forty seven thousand prime young harps on board and that we had the record of the old *Neptune,* under the command of Captain Sammy Blandford, beaten. We all hoped we would turn out the even fifty thousand. We passed Cape Bonavista around 10 a.m. The lightkeeper signalled us, asking the number of seals we had on board, and Captain Kean replied with forty seven blasts of our steam whistle indicating that we had forty seven thousand. We rounded Cape St. Francis about 2 p.m. and from there to St. John's the water was very rough and sometimes the ship rolled rail under. A lot of this roll was because the ship had only been pounded off to take thirty thousand. Consequently the balance of almost twenty thousand harps was shifting back and forth and causing this unusual roll. Some of the passengers were seasick. I was feeling fine, not a bit sick, and enjoying the rough weather. We came through St. John's Narrows about 4 p.m., all flags flying, and docked at Bowring' south side premises. We found the *Viking,* under command of Captain William Bartlett, father of Captain Bob Bartlett of North Pole fame, laying alongside the wharf and discharging her full cargo of some twenty five thousand. Captain Bartlett always prosecuted the sealfishery in the Gulf and on this particular voyage, one of many which he had made, he was the first arrival.

There were hundreds if not thousands of people lined up on Bowring's southside premises to welcome us home. I knew a great number of these people. Included amongst the number was my father. I was leaning over the port rail as the ship was docking. Eventually, when we were moored up to the wharf and the gangway was placed in position, I stepped off the ship. I was greeted by many people who knew me, but particularly by men from Bowring's office with whom I had worked for one and a half years. Then I was ordered by my father to get my clothes, dirty and all as they were, and come with him to the Balmoral Hotel where I spent the night. After mass the next day, Sunday, we left for Cape Broyle by horse and buggy. Father would not permit me to stay in St. John's to help to discharge the cargo, as all other members of the crew were compelled to do. I could have obtained a job as official tallyman and would have received extra remuneration. Father said I must go home. These were his orders and they had to be carried out. He scoffed at the idea of me going to sea on the *Rosalind* as I had arranged with Captain Williams. I must go back to Cape Broyle and work at the business. So home I went without a murmur. Nevertheless, I still had it in the back of my head to get out of Cape Broyle as soon as possible. When the cargo of seals was discharged from the *Florizel*, it turned out nearly fifty thousand young harps. To be accurate, the exact number was 49,069. The crew of 203 men shared $148.36 each. My money was collected by my father. That particular sealing year, the firm of Bowring Brothers secured upwards of one hundred and forty thousand seals for the seven ships which prosecuted the industry.

I enjoyed the trip to the sealfishery very much indeed. I enjoyed working with the various types of men who comprised the crew of that fine vessel. They were a sturdy lot. They were really specially selected men. Captain Abraham Kean, whilst he was fortunate in striking good voyages of seals, was not particularly popular with his men. He was very arrogant and most intolerant. I remember one morning, when some of the crew were slow getting out on the ice, others being sick with colds, Captain Kean roared through the sleeping quarters in an awful rage. It looked for a while as if there would be trouble, but, fortunately, the men concerned cooled down and conditions became normal. Captain Kean's son, Wesley, who was second hand with his father, was much more popular with the crew. Generally speaking, the men were residents of the north side of Bonavista Bay and any relations I might have had with them were most cordial.

Father and myself arrived back in Cape Broyle on Sunday afternoon, April 1st, 1910. On the way over the road we stopped at Bay Bulls at the home of a fine old gentleman named Philip Williams ("Long Phil"). Three miles further on we went down to see my Grandmother Mullowney at Witless Bay and to have the usual meal. Grandma was charmed to see me looking so well and also charmed that I had enjoyed my trip to the sealfishery. Then we could not pass through Tors Cove without paying the usual visit to our old and loyal friend, Pierre Ronayne, as well as some other old timers, who were great political supporters of my father. We arrived back in Cape Broyle just before dark. Mother was delighted to see me and well do I remember her ordering me to go out in the old cellar, take a bath and change my clothes. She said that I smelled of seal oil. I met many of the old-time fisher-men the following Monday and the general topic of discussion was: how did I get on at the ice? They all commented on the fact that the cargo we had procured was the biggest on record and that certainly I was no "jinker." I was feeling fine, physically, and now I had to settle down again to the general routine of preparing for the prosecution of the codfishery in 1910. Supplies of all kinds had to be brought from St. John's. We were preparing our own coaster, *Mary,* for the job of freighting these supplies during the summer months. In addition, as usual, we were compelled to hire other coasters to assist in this work. The skipper of the *Mary* was the late Tom Harvey of Admirals Cove, Cape

Broyle, father of Jack Harvey, to whom I have already referred in this chapter. His crew consisted of two other men besides himself. They had at least a month's work getting the old *Mary* ready.

The month of April was not long slipping by and as May month was generally a clean-up period, we were kept busy cleaning up around the premises, as well as around the house. Mother, who was now practically in full charge, was always adding new additions to the home. The roof of the house had been raised from a flat one to a saddle roof, the back kitchen had been raised in order to accommodate some of our employees. This work was done under the supervision of mother herself. Will Battcock from Brigus South, a first cousin of my father, was always the man in charge of these jobs. He was a blacksmith by trade, but was really a genius. He was a jack-of-all-trades. If anything went out of order at any time during the year, it was always Will Battcock who was engaged to repair it.

The last part of May we were kept busy giving general supplies to our main dealers to enable them to prosecute the codfishery. Our old and loyal blubber and oil man, Mr. Larry O'Neill had now become so old that he was unable to work any longer. He was a difficult man to replace. Finally, his job went to another man, Peter O'Brien, who had been salter with us during the trap voyage in previous years and who was a first cousin of my father. He, together with Jack Harvey, Stephen Carew and sometimes myself, was kept busy getting our blubber puncheons ready for the storage of rotten fish liver when the fishery began and particularly around the end of June when the Nova Scotia vessels, prosecuting the Bank fishery, came to Cape Broyle for ice, bait and other supplies. Peter was a very religious man. He had his hands full keeping us three young men in order, on many occasions. Our ice houses had already been filled with ice and we had to send the *Mary* to Colinet in St. Mary's Bay for a load of sawdust to spread over the ice to keep it from melting. All these things had to be done and our noses were kept to the grinding stone at all times.

Finally the summer of 1910 came around, our dealers

were all ready for the prosecution of the codfishery and, as I remember, that particular season was a profitable one for all concerned. Fish averaged around five dollars per quintal and a barrel of flour was generally looked upon as costing the price of an average quintal of fish. There was no such thing those days as flour in sacks. The Nova Scotia bank fishing fleet were doing well and came to land every week or ten days for their usual supply of ice, bait, etc. Mother was in full charge of the business at Cape Broyle. She went to town frequently, either over the road or by coastal boat, to purchase dry goods and other commodities with which father was unfamiliar. Father himself was in St. John's, being occupied with his high cabinet post of Minister of Finance and Customs. He looked after the purchase of flour, pork, beef, molasses, salt and other heavy commodities. He usually came home to Cape Broyle on weekends and inspected everything around the premises and house. God help you if anything was out of order.

Then when the month of August came around, or the early part of September, I was sent to buy dry codfish in Aquaforte, Ferryland and other places along the shore. This was my second summer at this particular job. It was my duty to see that the fish was properly culled and loaded into various coasters, and that it was dispatched to St. John's as early as possible. Father looked after the sale of this fish and I was always proud to find that it turned out a good profit. I had now been working at the Cashin enterprise at Cape Broyle for three summers. During these three seasons I worked from daylight until dark at all kinds of labour. For the years 1909-10 I was permitted to look after the sale of goods in the shop and store as well as take care of the accounts of banking vessels and our local fishermen dealers. I had not received one cent of remuneration, nor was I ever given or allowed an annual salary. I did receive my food, clothing and tobacco. When the annual fancy fair (garden party, today) for the church came around about the middle of August, I was given two or three dollars to spend.

The autumn season of 1910 was fast approaching and

we were kept going from daylight until dark at our various work, such as the handling of codfish in the several processes it has to go through before it is really ready for market. We were loading coasting boats with codfish taken in from our local dealers as well as shipping cod oil accumulated during the summer and autumn months. I had been talking to several old timers, personal friends of mine, like old Skipper Mickey ("Chips") O'Brien, my father's godfather, old Mr. John Dalton, "Gassy" as we all called him behind his back, and my great friend and cousin, Carrie Best, about the prospects of going to Canada and the opportunities there might be there for personal advancement. All these kind personal friends of mine were more than sympathetic towards me and I can assure my readers that their advice was of great help to me in later years. Also, during the summer of 1910, the survey and initial work on the construction of the Trepassey branch railway had begun.

As I have already pointed out in this chapter, the Morris government was confirmed in office by the general election held during the spring of 1909. One of the policies of that party pertained to the building of branch railways in certain parts of the island. It came to pass, therefore, that my father, now Minister of Finance of Newfoundland, with considerable influence in the government, was in a position to have that government agree to build a branch railway along the Southern Shore, through Ferryland district, extending into Trepassey which was a part of the district of Placentia and St. Mary's. The Reid Newfoundland Company was awarded the contract, not alone to construct the Ferryland-Trepassey branch railway, but also the Bonavista branch and a further extension of the Carbonear branch down to Bay de Verde. Sir William Reid, who was president of the Reid Newfoundland Company at that time, was a strong supporter of the Morris party. In fact he was bitterly opposed to the Bond administration. Further, I am confident it was the Reid Company, through Sir William Reid, which helped to find the necessary campaign funds to finance the two elections for the

Morris party in 1908-09. As fate would have it, I was not to be in Newfoundland for the completion of the building of the Trepassey branch railway.

There is an old saying, and I am convinced now that it is a true saying, that: "All work and no play makes Jack a dull boy." What recreation if any did I have during these three years at Cape Broyle? To begin with we were working every day practically from daylight until dark. Once in a while there would be the occasional outport dance, the music being supplied by the local fiddler, the blind fiddler from the Goulds or one of the many accordion players, of whom there are many in nearly all these outport communities. Such events would generally be on a Sunday or probably Saturday night. Other times, particularly after Christmas, there would be the occasional wedding to which one would be invited. Frequently we had the nightly game of cards, the old game of forty-fives, which we played at a couple of private homes, the stakes generally being small chews of tobacco, called at that time in the outports, "gumbeens." There were no such things as athletic games — no such things as movie pictures as we find in nearly all the outports today. Furthermore, when I did happen to go, or be permitted to go, to one of these private social entertainments, there was a strict rule laid down in our home that I was to be back in the house not later than 10 p.m. Once in a while I might get the horse and buggy on Sunday afternoon and pay a visit to friends in Calvert and Ferryland. I remember well making such visits to Captain Andrew Keough of Calvert. Captain Andy was a wonderful friend of my father, both politically and socially, and Mrs. Keough was always very kind and hospitable. Jim Keough of Calvert is a son of the late Captain Keough and attended St. Bonaventure's College in my later years there. Then there might be other visits to Ferryland on Sundays where I generally went down to Mike White's and paid social calls. We had two horses and buggies at that time and I considered it a great privilege to be permitted to take one of them on a Sunday afternoon to go for a drive to either of the places I have mentioned. On very infrequent occasions I might get the opportunity of going down to Witless Bay to see my Grandmother Mullowney. This was a distance of some eighteen miles from Cape Broyle.

There were certain places to which I was forbidden to go to social functions, even though the places concerned were owned by my father's greatest friends and political supporters. There were many times, when the opportunity arose, that I did not live up to these home regulations. The violation of this particular regulation was what finally brought on, or was responsible for, my getting out of Cape Broyle as well as Newfoundland. One particular evening there was a social dance at a house in Shore's Cove, which is located a distance of about one and a half miles from our home at Cape Broyle. Myself and Jack Harvey, who was still working with us and living at our house, knew that this particular social event was to take place. After supper, we both walked down to Shore's Cove to join with others in this particular entertainment. Father and mother were both at home at this particular time. I knew I had to be back home not later than 10 p.m., but by some oversight on my part, it was around 10:30 p.m. when I arrived back at our house in Cape Broyle. Father was in bed and so were the several maids that were working with us. This was in the early part of October, 1910. I noticed when I was walking across the road towards our house that the lamps were turned out in the front rooms, but one was still shining in the kitchen. I had walked at great speed from Shore's Cove. When, eventually, I arrived in the kitchen, mother asked me where I had been and I· told her the truth. She then told me that father was very annoyed and that he would kill me the following morning. When I use the word "kill", I do not mean it to be construed as actual murder. I mean to convey that, according to my mother's words, father had it in his head to beat me the following morning.

I went to bed immediately but did not sleep. I was thinking over in my mind what would happen in the morning. I knew from personal experience the violent and uncontrollable temper with which my respected father was unfortunately afflicted. So, I made up my mind to be out of Cape Broyle before he arose. I decided to get out of bed around two or, at the latest, three a.m. This I did, and crept downstairs in my stocking feet, making no noise. I put on my boots and went out of the house by the back kitchen door. Then I decided to walk to Witless Bay. I was going back to my beloved old Grandmother Mullowney, who had reared me until I was ten years old.

When I came to the outskirts of Tors Cove, a distance of some twelve miles from Cape Broyle, which took me nearly four hours and without any food, I decided to walk through the woods on the outskirts of both Tors Cove and Mobile, so that people would not see me. After passing Mobile I again took to the main road and continued on to Witless Bay, arriving there in the afternoon. I went directly to Grandmother Mullowney's house and told her and Uncle Louis the story of what had happened the night before.

It transpired that when father and mother arose from their bed that morning and missed me, they became worried, coming to the conclusion that I had gone to Witless Bay. They then telegraphed my Uncle Louis to bring me back and that everything would be alright. Uncle Louis acquainted me of this particular telegram and very reluctantly I returned to Cape Broyle with him by horse and carriage. My uncle further assured me that if father lost his temper with me I could return with him again to Witless Bay. After having a real good meal, because I was certainly hungry, myself and Uncle Louis set out for Cape Broyle. I felt safe so long as he was with me.

We arrived at Cape Broyle around 10 p.m. Father and Mother were glad to see me back. Uncle Louis stayed all night and returned to Witless Bay the following morning. As usual I arose early the next day. Father was nice to me and asked me to do certain work which I set about doing. He returned to St. John's himself the following day. Mother talked with me during the day and told me that both herself and father had agreed to let me go away to Canada, and that father was going to see Sir William Reid on his return to St. John's, requesting him to get in contact with some of his many friends in Montreal with the object of getting me a job. I was now full of hope for the future. I felt that Sir William Reid, at that time with considerable influence in financial circles in Montreal, would be able to have me placed in some kind of a decent occupation.

In the meantime, mother began preparing new clothes for me and getting everything ready for my great adventure in the fast-growing Dominion of Canada. Canada at that period had a population of less than eight million people. I felt that I was now to be set free — that I would be able to do as I saw fit — that I would have a certain liberty of action which I had not been accustomed to in either St. John's or Cape Broyle. I continuously talked to my old-timer friends around Cape Broyle, Calvert and Ferryland. Naturally, I paid a special visit to my dear old Grandmother Mullowney at Witless Bay. I told her of my new-found prospects and left her that particular evening with tears in her eyes and a prayer on her lips for her own boy, Peter. In all, I was most optimistic for the future. I had read in the newspapers the statement of the then Prime Minister of Canada, Sir Wilfred Laurier, ''That the twentieth century belonged to Canada.''

Finally the news arrived through Sir William Reid that I was to be given a position with the Royal Securities Corporation of Montreal, and that I should leave for there as early as possible. I said goodbye to all my good and loyal friends at Cape Broyle and proceeded to St. John's by the S.S. *Portia,* still under the command of Captain Thomas Fitzpatrick. We docked at Bowring's north side premises late in the afternoon around the middle of November, 1910, and I went to the Balmoral Hotel for a few days. Mother came to St. John's with me and as father was staying with my Aunt Jane Mullowney, who lived on Prescott Street, mother went there.

The following day father took me up to meet Sir William Reid, who gave me a letter of introduction to Mr. B.A. McNab, then editor-in-chief of the *Montreal Star.* Sir William told me that Mr. McNab had arranged this particular job for me, and that I need not worry, as I would be placed as promised. Father then bought my railway ticket and sleeper for me to Montreal, which at that time cost in the vicinity of fifty dollars. I had earned $148.36 at the sealfishery in the *Florizel* during the spring of 1910, so my transportation costs to Montreal were deducted from this amount and I was handed the balance of around ninety dollars, which was my cash capital to start in the world anew. I was now ready to leave for my great Canadian adventure.

Chapter 4

I Migrate To Canada

On a Thursday evening at 6 p.m., about the last half of November, 1910, I boarded the Newfoundland cross country express train, to, first of all, cross the island of Newfoundland to Port-aux-Basques, a distance of almost five hundred and fifty miles. It may be of interest to my readers to know that at that time the cross country express took twenty-six hours to get to Port-aux-Basques from St. John's and that, in its last years of service, it took twenty-seven hours. The roadbed of the railway was not in particularly good condition and the entire system across the island was railed with fifty pound steel. It was, in fact, the first time I had really been on a railway train, apart from the occasional excursion on a Sunday afternoon during the summers of 1906-07 as far as Donovans, a distance from the city of St. John's of about five miles. Father, Mother, Aunt Jane Mullowney, my brothers, Dick and Martin, who were boarders at St. Bonaventure's College, as well as my sister Mary, who was staying with Aunt Jane and going to school at the Mercy Convent, were at the station to see me off. Father had introduced me to a Mr. Phelan, who had been down in Newfoundland on behalf of the firm of H. R. Silver and Company of Halifax buying codfish and who was returning to Halifax. Mr. Phelan was a great help to me in every respect. It was he who gave me some idea of the road I was about to travel.

As that train, which was composed of a couple of sleeping cars, a dining car, two or three ordinary passenger cars, as well as a baggage and mail car, pulled out on time from the railway station, I, together with Mr. Phelan, stood on the tail end of the rear sleeping car and waved goodbye to all the members of my family. Once we pulled out of the present railway station and began chugging our way towards Waterford Bridge, I felt myself beginning to breathe free air. I had about eighty or ninety dollars of actual cash in my pocket. I felt I was now headed for a great commercial and financial future. Mr. Phelan and I had dinner or supper on that train. At that time I thought it was a wonderful experience to be able to ride on what I then considered was a most modern and comfortable means of transportation. In my inexperienced mind, I really thought that the speed of this mode of conveyance was miraculous. In fact it is evident that later, under the supposedly efficient management of the Canadian National Railways, with all the new equipment, with more powerful and heavier locomotives, with better ballasted roadbeds and the rerailing of the entire cross-country system with seventy pound steel, it took longer for an express train to cross the island.

After supper we went out in the smoking compartment of the sleeping car. We talked with other passengers and now I was really free to enjoy my pipe as never before in my lifetime. It was now dark and I was unable to see what kind of country we were moving through. I did learn, however, that this express train, the most modern and luxurious form of transportation ever introduced into Newfoundland, was rolling along like our old coaster, *Mary*, in a calm swell in the middle of Cape Broyle Bay. In fact there were times when one would think that this future *Newfie Express* would overturn. We retired to our sleepers about midnight. It was my first time to rest and slumber in a railway sleeping car. We arrived at Bishops Falls early the following morning and I arose to have a look at this western divisional centre of the Reid Newfoundland Company's railway operations. It was at that time almost a wilderness, with the exception of a small pulp mill being operated by the Anglo-Newfoundland Development Company. The Grand Falls station was nothing better than a flag station. There were very few residents in the territory now known as the town of Windsor. The little town of Grand Falls was a couple of miles from the railway station, and we could see the smoke from the stack of the then modern paper mill, recently constructed through the pioneering spirit of the Harmsworth Brothers, producing somewhere in the vicinity of one hundred tons of newsprint daily.

Moving west from Grand Falls, passing Badger and Millertown, stopping at each place for a few minutes, we ultimately came to the foot of the Gaff Topsails. The weather was cold. There was no snow yet to be seen on this most rugged part of the Island of Newfoundland. Slowly we climbed the steep grade, and I was able to see for myself the loneliness and isolation of the people employed by the Reid Company to keep this so-called modern railway in actual operation. When this train ultimately arrived at the peak of the Gaff Topsails, it was then I was able to see the majestic grandeur in the ruggedness of the surrounding mountains. For the first time in my life I began to realize to myself, what a beautiful part of Newfoundland I had just left. Because now as I was about to leave this rock-bound island, I became aware of the scenic beauty of Tors Cove just twelve miles from Cape Broyle, the narrow, winding road over which I had so frequently driven by horse and buggy. I began thinking about what a beautiful place LeManche was, where old Skipper Paddy Crane and his hospitable wife, Mary Anne, lived in isolation, where one could see as the sun was setting in the west, a replica of the Lakes of Killarney in the flowing river and lake. Then I became conscious of the beautiful harbour of Cape Broyle, the place where I was born, a settlement I now had left and might never see again. I could see its picturesque form as one approached it from the south, coming to the top of the south side hill. Then I thought of that natural harbour of Aquaforte, where I had spent so many happy hours at the hospitable home of Yankee Bill Croft and Mrs. Croft. I thought of the historic settlement of Ferryland, where Baltimore landed in the sixteenth century and which prides itself on the independent spirit of its people. I thought of my sweet old Grandmother Mullowney in Witless Bay, whom I knew was praying for me. Yes, I thought of all these things and places, and was looking forward now to more wonderful things to come. Then as we headed down on the western side of the Gaff Topsails, it looked dreary and lonely. There were no such places as Howley or Deer Lake. Nothing could be seen which would attract the eye until we arrived at the head of the Humber River. The splendour of the winding, romantic Humber was a sight most beautiful to behold. Then we arrived at Humbermouth, another divisional point on the would-be modern transportation system where engines were changed for the final lap of the journey to Port-aux-Basques. Mr. Phelan and myself took a little exercise by walking back and forth on the old wooden platform.

We had breakfast between Grand Falls and Humbermouth and the dinner hour was approaching when I would have my last meal of Newfoundland codfish for several years. We pulled out from Humbermouth on time. There was nothing at Corner Brook at that time except the old Fisher lumber mill. We stopped a few minutes at Curling and had a beautiful view of the picturesque Bay of Islands. We approached the beautiful Codroy Valley during the afternoon and one could see the many small farms and salmon rivers — rivers world famous for their salmon fishing at certain periods of the year. Finally, we arrived at Port-aux-Basques, the terminal of this wonderful railway — wonderful in my mind at any rate, because I had never been on a railway before. It was the connecting link between Newfoundland and Canada. It was now around 8 p.m. on a bleak November evening in 1910. We were now to transfer ourselves and our luggage aboard the old steamer *Bruce,* under the command at that time, I think, of Captain Delaney. We had to go through the usual red tape of giving particulars of ourselves to the purser of the ship. This information would be handed over to the immigration officer at North Sydney on our arrival there. We pulled out from the pier around 9 p.m. and made the crossing to the mainland of Canada, a distance of a little over one hundred miles, in about eight or nine hours. I can now visualize myself, as something of a Napoleon, standing on the after quarter of the *Bruce,* with my hands behind my back, my head erect, and my mind saying goodbye for ever to dear old Newfoundland.

When I set foot on Canadian soil that Saturday morning I became an immigrant. All the passengers had to line up and give their story to the immigration officer, whom I must say was most kind and considerate to me. Mr. Phelan was a great help to me in showing me the ropes and the way I had to get on board that Canadian train, operated at that time by the Intercolonial Railway Company between the Maritime provinces and Montreal. I satisfied the Canadian officer in question as to my qualifications for remaining in Canada, as I already had the promise of a permanent job. In this respect I was to find out sooner than I thought that promises are made to be broken. It never dawned on me that morning that in less than a year I would find myself moving west to grow up with the country and eventually spend Christmas, 1911, in that beautiful city of Victoria, British Columbia.

We left North Sydney around 9 a.m. and immediately I became conscious of the difference between the Newfoundland express train on which I had crossed the island, and this Canadian train, the cars and engines of which were much larger and more luxurious than those which were operated over that narrow gauge, rickety roadbed of the then Newfoundland railway. The trip from North Sydney to Truro occupied about twelve hours. I had anticipated seeing more wonderful scenery and beautiful homes, now that I had come to this fast-growing Dominion. To be quite frank, I was more than disappointed. The territory through which that Intercolonial train travelled from Sydney to Truro did not greatly impress me. I had never known people live in such hovels as could at that time be found in the mining areas of Cape Breton and parts of the province of Nova Scotia. There was nothing like that to be seen in dear old Newfoundland. We had breakfast in what appeared to me to be a sumptuous railway dining car. The meals, whilst nicely served, were not to be compared to those supplied on the old Reid Newfoundland Railway, even though the seats were more comfortable and the progress of the train smoother. I was particularly interested when we arrived at Port Mulgrave, where the train was split into two parts and ferried across from Cape Breton to Nova Scotia on a special steam ferry. It was to me at that time a feat of great engineering ingenuity. Finally we arrived at Truro, where I parted from Mr. Phelan and joined another train which was to bring me to Montreal, the metropolis of Canada — a great city with a population at that time of somewhere in the vicinity of six or seven hundred thousand people.

This particular train which I joined at Truro was the direct train from Halifax to Montreal, where we were scheduled to arrive on a Sunday evening around 8 p.m. The weather was much colder and snow covered the ground. All night long we sped over that standard gauge railway at a speed of over thirty miles per hour. I was out of my sleeper early and found my way to the dining car where I breakfasted. I stared through the windows of that large sleeping car all day, viewing with the keenest of interest the surrounding country. We were by now coming to the boundary line of the province of Quebec which adjoins the province of New Brunswick. When we would stop to change engines at divisional points, I would get off and exercise myself walking up and down the platforms. I knew no one in this vast country. I was interested in hearing a new language spoken, particularly after entering the province of Quebec. Then we came to the south shore of the St. Lawrence river. I did not see in this new land which I was now entering, the natural beauty I had left behind me in Newfoundland. We arrived at Point Levis, which is right opposite the historic city of Quebec on the South Shore of the St. Lawrence river. It was about four o'clock in the afternoon. From here we could see the spot where Wolfe landed and died centuries before as he led the small British Army to take this part of French Canada for Britain. The St. Lawrence river was still open to navigation, although ice was forming on its flowing waters. As we rode through this quaint province, dotted on all sides with thatch-roofed cottages and farm houses, owned and operated by French Canadian farmers, I felt that I was approaching something or some place which held in reserve a special storehouse filled with happiness and prosperity. After we left Levis, the train seemed to pick up speed and after a period of around five hours arrived in the great city of Montreal.

Before I left St. John's the previous Thursday

evening, I had been told by my father that Jim Fox, stepson of Sir Edward Morris, would meet me at the Montreal terminal, at the foot of Windsor Street, which was then known as Bonaventure station. After tipping the porter in the customary manner, I stepped down to the terminal platform of that station expecting Fox to be there. I had known him personally from the first year I was at St. Bonaventure's College and later met him when he was working in the Bank of Montreal at St. John's. He was now working with the same bank in Montreal and was rooming with the Misses Vinicombe on Park Avenue. I waited around to meet Fox, but he never turned up. I felt kind of lost in this great big railway terminal. I was a real "greenhorn." What was I to do? I decided that I would follow the crowd through the station and look for some place to stay for the night. To be truthful, I was bewildered. I prayed to God to guide me. Much to my surprise, I was so fortunate in a few minutes as to run into a Mr. McCaffrey, who had been in St. John's during the two seasons I was working at Bowring's and who had operated a roller skating business in the old Princess rink. He knew me and, as he came from Montreal, he realized my predicament. He was most kind. He put me on board a horse-drawn sleigh and advised me to go to the old Leland Hotel, located on McGill College Avenue above St. Catherine Street. When I arrived at this hotel, which is now non-existent, I registered in the usual way, advising the room clerk that I would be staying there for a couple of days. The first thing I did was to telephone Jim Fox at Miss Vinicombe's house and tell him of my arrival. He came over to see me immediately and took me out to meet Mrs. LeBel and her husband. Mrs. LeBel was the sister of Sir Edward Morris and she had arranged a boarding house for me where I could go the following day. I also met the Misses Vinicombe and Miss Reardon, the three of whom were always kind to me during the period I was to live in Montreal.

The following morning, Monday, I engaged a horse and sleigh and asked the driver to take me to the office of the *Montreal Star*. I wanted to present my letter of introduction from Sir William Reid to Mr. B. A. McNab.

I distinctly remember entering this building, located on St. James Street West, and honestly I was amazed. I had never seen anything like this in my life. How could I? I had never been out of Newfoundland. The printing presses were rolling and the first edition of the *Daily Star* was being prepared. I asked one of the clerks at the front counter could I see Mr. McNab, as I had a letter of introduction to him. I was shown to the elevator, the first time I had been in such a means of communication in my life. Finally I arrived at the floor where Mr. McNab's office was located. Again I asked one of the clerks or reporters for Mr. McNab and finally was ushered into McNab's private office, presenting him with Sir William Reid's letter of introduction. That particular office floor was humming with activity. Reporters and editors were pounding out their usual stories on typewriters, preparing their good or bad news for the publication of the final daily edition of this great Canadian newspaper. Mr. McNab received me most courteously. We talked at first about Newfoundland and Sir William Reid. Then we came to the most important matter — the job I was to get with the Royal Securities Company. Mr. McNab told me to come and see him the following morning, Tuesday, and he would take me over to see the general manager of the Bank of Montreal. He then took me to lunch at the old Freeman's Hotel, which at that time was located opposite the *Star* office, on St. James Street. We had a very nice lunch and a general talk about Newfoundland affairs, and I returned to the old Leland Hotel.

Feeling certain at that time of a fairly good position, I immediately moved my trunk and other belongings to my new boarding house, arranged for me by Mrs. LeBel, and located on the north corner of Sherbrooke and St. Denis Streets. This particular boarding house was operated by French people. All the other roomers and boarders were French. The charge for my room and board was thirty dollars per month payable in advance. After paying this monthly payment, I now had a net cash capital of less than fifty dollars in my pocket. I roamed around the streets, being amazed at the grandeur of the stores and the residences. I became homesick. I met no one on any of the streets whom I knew. However, I had made my decision and was determined to face whatever obstacles came in my path in a manly and honest manner. Surely, I thought in my own mind, that in this growing country, which now had a total population of around eight millions of people, I could make the grade. I had supper. Not one person in that large dining room spoke a word of English and I can assure my readers that my knowledge of French was anything but perfect. I went to bed early and looked forward to the following morning (Tuesday) and this newfound way of life which I had anticipated.

I arose early that Tuesday morning. I had read the *Montreal Daily Star* the night previous and it was not until then that I came to realize that there was such a thing as "seasonal unemployment." I had struck Montreal at the wrong time of year. Nevertheless, I felt in my own mind that I would be placed in a job, as surely this man McNab who had been built up to me by Sir William Reid, was not fooling me. I was at his office at 9:30 a.m. I did not need to ask anyone where his office was located this time. I was able to find my own way to the particular office floor where he was located. Again I was ushered into his private "sanctum-sanctorum." Mr. McNab telephoned some secretary or other at the Bank of Montreal and shortly we walked east on St. James Street to this headquarters of Canada's leading financial institution. We were met by a secretary attired in morning clothes, who announced our arrival to Sir Frederick Williams-Taylor, then general manager of this great bank. I was less than twenty-one years old and one can imagine the conversation which took place. Sir Frederick asked about my father and Sir Edward Morris, but there was no mention about any kind of a job. Mr. McNab told me after that interview to see him in a few days' time, and after about a week going back and forth to his office, he finally arranged some kind of a job for me with the French newspaper *La Patrie.* It was owned and controlled by a French Canadian family named Tarte. I heard no more about the Royal Securities Company. I started work in that office about December 1st, 1910, making out English invoices, which were very few. Generally speaking I could see that there was nothing of any consequence in this place. Of the several scores of employees in that organization only two of us were English-speaking and the other English-speaking gentleman spoke French fluently.

One day Mr. Tarte called me to his private office and suggested that I make an effort to get the Newfoundland government to give their paper a big advertisement to be written in French, which would be for the purpose of advertising the tourist possibilities in Newfoundland for the French Canadian people. I wrote my father on the matter, but his reply was in the negative. I told Mr. Tarte of the reply I had received and his attitude was not particularly friendly, so I made up my mind to try and get another job on my own. My month was nearly expired where I was boarding and my wages were fourteen dollars per week. I figured out I could not afford to stay there another month. I had now begun to learn that although people might appear friendly and polite, I was just one individual amongst half a million others in a world in which everyone had to look after himself. And further, I became aware, to use a saying that developed in later years, that I was getting the "brush-off" from so-called friends.

Christmas was now fast approaching and I decided to hang on to the French newspaper job until after the holiday season had ended. I was invited to Christmas dinner by Mr. and Mrs. LeBel. They were wonderfully kind to me. There were many nights I was invited there to play cards with them and the Misses Vinicombe and Miss Reardon. I very seldom saw Jim Fox. There was nothing for me to see him about. He could do nothing for me in any case, as he had no more influence than myself.

In the meantime, I ran into Mr. Frank Jackman, who was at that time buyer for the Scroggie firm which operated a big departmental store on the corner of Windsor and St. Catherine Streets, where the fine new Dominion Square building is located today. Through Frank Jackman, whom I knew as a boy in Newfoundland, I found a few other Newfoundlanders like myself, struggling to make their way in the big city. I had met Frank English, whom I had gone to school with at St. Bonaventure's College. Frank was the son of the late Captain Edward English Sr., harbour master of St. John's at that time. His brother, Captain Edward English Jr., later succeeded his father, but was at that time master of the Customs cutter *Fiona*. Then I met Jack O'Reilly, whom I also had known in Newfoundland, when he was a member of the Irish Society as well as a member of the Catholic cadet band.

The three of us, then very young, I was probably the youngest of the three, decided that we would try and get room and board in the same house. This resulted in my moving from the very nice French boarding house to another boarding house on Lagauchetiere Street West, near Windsor Street, where O'Reilly, English and myself obtained room and board for four dollars and fifty cents per week. The three of us shared the one large room, with three comfortable beds. The food, though plain, was very good. It was now about the middle of January, 1911. Having resigned my position with the French newspaper, *La Patrie,* I was looking for a job and jobs were anything but plentiful at that particular time of year.

O'Reilly was working as a clerk with the Grand Trunk Railway, having obtained this job through the good influences of a Jesuit priest named Father Doyle, at that time associated with Ste. Marie College on Bleury Street. English was working as a clerk in one of the accounting departments of the Canadian Pacific Railway, having come over to Canada from New York a year or so previously. Jack O'Reilly suggested that he would take me down to meet Father Doyle. Father Doyle was a great personal friend of one of the secretaries of Sir Thomas Shaughnessey, president of the Canadian Pacific Railway. He telephoned this particular gentleman and gave me a note of introduction to him. Almost immediately I received an appointment as a stenographer in the staff records department of that great private corporation, at a salary of forty dollars per month. I brushed up on my shorthand and typewriting and before many days passed was able to hammer out all the letters and memoranda the chief clerk of that department could dictate to me. While the salary was small, the job served its purpose. It gave me a chance to look around. It meant security. It gave me an opportunity of sizing up, from every angle, this great city, and the possibilities for the future. It also, in a general way, allowed me to try and educate myself to this new Canadian way of life.

O'Reilly and English had been in Canada a year or two before I arrived to take the place by storm. At night time we generally talked about the possibilities for the future. O'Reilly was concentrating his efforts on singing. Occasionally, one of us who might have acquired some social friends might be invited to their homes for dinner on Sunday. In this respect I must pay special tribute to Mr. and Mrs. Charles Wadden, who lived on Durocher Street and who were most kind and hospitable towards me. Mr. Wadden came from St. John's and had been living in Montreal for many years. Neither O'Reilly, English or myself were being paid exorbitant salaries and we did not have much money to spend on wild living. We occasionally might go to a moving picture show (silent) and, very infrequently, had the opportunity of seeing some musical comedy, play or vaudeville show from the gallery of one of the theatres, then familiarly known as the "gods." I had yet to take my first drink of alcoholic beverage and neither one of these particular friends of mine drank to excess at any time. We attended to our religious duties regularly at St. Patrick's church. I never missed a week during which I did not write to my mother and she too was equally prompt in writing to me. A letter from home in those days meant a lot. Sometimes we received the Newfoundland newspapers and were able to keep ourselves informed of the happenings in the old land.

I kept working away at my job as stenographer in the staff records office of the Canadian Pacific Railway. I became very efficient at this job. I arrived at the stage where I could take down one hundred and fifty words per minute in dictation and transcribe it back with that old Empire typewriter in quick time. There did not appear to me to be much possibility for advancement in this particular branch of the railway organization. On Saturdays we generally had a half holiday. So, one Saturday afternoon I walked into the head distributing office of the Smith Premier Typewriting Company and enquired of the manager if there were any possibilities for experienced stenographers or typists that he knew of. He immediately informed me, after I had told him where I was working, that there was a possibility of obtaining employment in the operation of a new style of billing machine with the wholesale dry goods firm of McIntyre Sons & Co., Ltd., located in a large building in downtown Montreal. He gave me a test and felt that I was suitable for the job. The following Monday I got an hour off from work and, with a note from the manager of the typewriting company, had an interview with the particular supervisor of this new department being set up by this drygoods firm. I was successful in getting the job and was advised to report for work in two weeks' time. Then I returned to the chief clerk of the C.P.R. staff records office and tendered my resignation. I was to receive a salary in this new position of fifteen dollars weekly to start with, a considerable advance over the paltry forty dollars per month I was being paid by this great Canadian Pacific Railway Company.

Around May the 1st, 1911, I began work at my new job. It was a new system of making out invoices by a special kind of typewriter. I became very good at the work and felt I would make favourable progress in this business. This new job, which paid me fifty percent more salary than I had been receiving from the C.P.R., enabled me to get a little more pleasure and recreation out of life. Frequently now I attended the nightly shows, either the movies or vaudeville, and Saturday evenings during the early part of the summer, I enjoyed going to Dominion Park to ride the various contraptions and play the various games which, to me at that time, were a great source of pleasure. These things gave me a certain recreation to which I had not been accustomed in Newfoundland. Frank English and Jack O'Reilly generally came along with me and together we got a great "kick" out of the whole business. In later years I learned to look upon such entertainment as a mere fleecing of the public.

At that particular period the Canadian Pacific Railway were giving every encouragement to British and other European peoples to come to Canada and settle on farm lands, which that company had acquired through agreements they had made with the Canadian government when building the railway across Canada. The Canadian government at that time was making special preparations to receive these future Canadians, who came principally from Great Britain, the Scandinavian countries and from many other countries of Europe. The passenger ships arriving in Montreal after the opening of navigation in May were crowded with these people, who were imbued with the idea of making their fortunes in this now fast-expanding Dominion of Canada. Special trains were assigned to carry these people to the various parts of Canada, but particularly to the prairie provinces, and British Columbia. It was about this time that Sir Wilfred Laurier, then Prime Minister of Canada, returned from the Imperial Conference in London. I had the great privilege of listening to that greatest of Canadian statesmen speak to an open air meeting near the Montreal City Hall shortly after he disembarked from the ship which had taken him back to his own French Canada. I will never forget the great personality, the distinguished appearance of that silver-tongued orator. I can yet see his long white hair waving in the spring breeze as he spoke both in French and English to that huge gathering of Canadian people. He spoke of the great possibilities for the development of the prairie provinces, which I think were later termed the "bread basket" of the British Empire.

It was now about the first part of June, 1911. Frank English and myself discussed the possibilities that might be out West for a future. We were both in good physical condition. We felt we were able to handle any kind of a job and we knew from reading the various pamphlets and other literature regarding the potential development of the western part of Canada, that one had to be ready and capable of handling any kind of work which might be offering. We had ideas at first of working at the harvest and of later taking out a homestead on a plan where one could get 160 acres of land in most remote areas by the downpayment of about forty dollars, with the provision that one would live on that quarter section for six months each year and undertake to break ten acres of this virgin soil annually. We had visions of making our fortunes as farmers in the Golden West. Both of us eventually came to the decision that we would resign our positions as office workers in Montreal around the end of July, 1911, and take the harvesters' excursion train to any part of the West we desired. The fare was ten dollars per passage for a return railway ticket on the C.P.R. from Montreal to Moose Jaw, Saskatchewan. We kept our plans to ourselves and neither one of us informed our parents in Newfoundland of our great decision. The slogan at that time, or might I call it railway propaganda, was "Go West young man, go West and grow up with the country." We reserved our transportation on the C.P.R. to leave Montreal about August the 1st, 1911. We were to gamble our future in a great adventure.

M.P. Cashin

Grandmother "Moody" Mullowney

Gertrude Mullowney Cashin

Grandfather Pierre Mullowney

Aunt Essie Mullowney

Uncle Louis Mullowney

Gertrude Cashin, Mary, Martin, Larry, Richard

Sir Michael and Lady Gertrude Cashin

Major Peter Cashin

Michael Cashin (son)

Mrs. Mary Waller (daughter)

Chapter 5

I Move To Western Canada

Early in August, 1911, Frank English and I boarded one of the many harvester excursion trains which were leaving the C.P.R. Windsor Street station at intervals of every half hour or hour. These trains were made up of rough colonist cars, each car accommodating about forty men, who came from all parts of Eastern Canada, Great Britain and Europe. Many of us were taking advantage of the cheap rate of transportation to get to the west, whilst others, coming principally from the province of Ontario, would be returning to their homes again in the autumn as soon as the harvesting of the grain crop was completed.

We all have heard criticism of certain Newfoundland trains; a great number of us have travelled on these same Newfoundland trains. I have no hesitation in saying that the worst Newfoundland trains I have ever seen or travelled on in Newfoundland were pullman trains in comparison to these harvester excursion trains used to carry men to the prairie provinces of Canada in those days. There was no such thing as a dining or sleeping car. We had to fight to get our seats - had to carry most of our food with us and try to grab a cup of tea or coffee at the various railroad stations on the way to what we thought at that time was the "Golden West." Certainly the rate charged for passage was low. At the same time I have no doubt that the Federal government of Canada was subsidizing the Canadian Pacific Railway to do this work for the purpose of getting settlers into the great farming provinces of Manitoba, Saskatchewan and Alberta; or it may be that the Canadian Pacific Railway Company, which had been granted huge tracts of farming land by the government for building this trans-Canada railway, were making efforts to have their own land settled and its rich soil developed and brought into production.

Our particular train moved at a very low speed; it

was even slower than our Newfoundland system. We were side-tracked for nearly every kind of other train and were herded like cattle at the various stations where we would stop to change engines. It appears that in previous years great trouble had been caused by passengers on these harvester excursion trains at various stop stations or divisional points. This caused both the railway and civilian authorities to take certain precautions, so that we harvesters would not be permitted outside the station where we would stop for any unusually long period. Well do I remember our arrival at the great city of Winnipeg, which is the headquarters of the Canadian Pacific Railway in western Canada. The station platform and station itself were literally guarded by scores of police officers, and we were not even permitted to look through the main door of the railway terminal to have a glance at this fast-growing prairie city, which was to become one of the greatest grain-distributing centres in western Canada. In fact, Winnipeg today is one of the largest, if not the largest, railway terminal in all of Canada. If my memory serves me correctly we were delayed several hours at this particular point. After leaving here we passed through the great grain belt west of Winnipeg; and from there onwards it was quite a scene to see the expensive wheat fields, now all ready for the cutting and threshing of all kinds of grain in this great western centre of all Canada. The road-bed was as level as a billiard board. Our train picked up speed and as we crossed the borderline between the province of Manitoba and Saskatchewan we could see that in reality we were coming to a country which, particularly at that time, depended entirely on the success of the annual grain crop for its prosperity.

Finally we arrived at the city of Regina, the capital of the province of Saskatchewan, the seat of the provincial government and the headquarters of the Royal Canadian Mounted Police. It was then a small city of something less than thirty thousand people, but extensive civic work was being carried out which was to further expand and modernize this new and fast-growing capital. It was about three o'clock in the morning when our train pulled into the station of this grain-growing centre of the Dominion of Canada. English and myself had already decided to detrain at this point, a distance of almost two thousand miles from the city of Montreal. Under ordinary circumstances a passenger train would have covered this distance in around three days, but this harvester excursion train, which was not much better than a cattle train, took four or more days to cover the distance. A few other men from our train detrained here. We had been informed that a great number of men would be engaged from this centre to work at the threshing and general harvesting of the Saskatchewan grain crop. At that time the railway station at Regina was a very modest wooden building. It was impossible for us to find out where we could get a place to live for the night. So we decided to sleep it out on the floor of the railway station. We used our suitcases as pillows and lay down on the floor. As we were tired and dreary after this long and tedious journey, we were soon fast asleep. However, this comfort did not last very long, as soon the railway police ejected us from the building and we were forced to slumber on the park benches in front of the station for the remainder of the night. Fortunately the weather was warm and we did not suffer any discomfort in this respect. We were looking forward to contacting some labour agency or other in the morning and to being able to get out of the city and take part in the harvesting of the Canadian grain crop. Both English and myself were young and strong and were physically capable of handling any kind of strenuous work.

Well do I remember waking up on that park bench on that particular morning in the early part of August, 1911. I remember an old gentleman, a retired farmer I should say, coming to both of us young fellows and asking us if we would care to earn our breakfast. He wanted to know if we were able to milk a couple of cows. Even at that time, one could see that Regina was just in its infancy. We both agreed to take on the job and went with this old gentleman to a small barn behind his residence and performed the operation of milking his two cows. I would prefer not to say whether we did the job properly. Whilst I had witnessed the milking of cows at home in Cape Broyle, I had never actually performed the job myself; and now I must confess I do not think I did the job properly or efficiently. English was much more proficient than I was in this respect. Nevertheless, this old retired gentleman overlooked my deficiencies in this particular instance, and was kind enough to have both of us served with a good breakfast consisting of porridge, ham and eggs, tea or coffee. We then returned to the railway station, procured our suitcases and had a general clean-up in the men's lavatory, after which we felt as fit as fiddles. We were now on the way to seek employment in the gathering of Canada's great grain crop.

After leaving the railway station with the intention of investigating the possibilities for work, we ran into two former Newfoundlanders sitting in the small park-lot in front of the station, sunning themselves. They had been in western Canada for several years. One of them had been living in a monastery during the previous winter, whilst the other had been roaming around the west doing odd jobs. The picture they painted for us did not appear too bright. We talked with them before proceeding to one of the labour agencies, where we ascertained that the harvesting of the grain crop would not get into full swing for another week. However, the man in charge of the labour bureau informed us that there were other odd jobs which could be obtained if we were capable of doing the work. We both assured him that we were capable of doing any kind of work. So, off we went to a contractor, an American, who had the job from the municipality of hauling sand to various parts of the city, where extensive construction work was being carried out in the laying of sewage lines to further expand the supply of water to this fast-growing metropolis of Saskatchewan. English approached the foreman of the stables first and asked him if it was possible to get a job driving a team of horses. The foreman enquired of him whether he had any ex-perience in this kind of work and English assured him that he had driven a team of horses in New York and could manage the job with efficiency. He immediately obtained a job as a team driver and began work at once. I then approached this same individual asking him for a job. He asked me if I had ever driven a team of horses before. I informed him that I had never driven a team, but had considerable experience in handling horses at home in Newfoundland. He told me to come around the next morning.

Whilst English was at work and I must say doing a good job, showing his efficiency in the handling of a pair of horses, I went around and found a place for both of us to live that night. Eventually I settled for two cot beds in a canvas tent. The price we had to pay for our beds each night was twenty five cents. In addition, there was another large tent where we could obtain our meals for twenty five cents per meal. In all, our board and lodging would cost us one dollar per day. There were working men living there from all over Canada and the United States who were employed at various kinds of jobs. The accommodation was clean and the food was good, solid, workingmen's food. We were comfortable. The weather was warm, but nevertheless we were looking forward to being able to obtain employment at the harvesting of the grain crop, which was our objective when we left Montreal.

The following morning, after having a very good rest, we arose early, had breakfast and, together with English, I went to the barn to see if there was any possibility of getting the job the foreman had told me about the day before. I went to the foreman of that particular concern, reminding him that he had told me to show up this morning as there might be a chance of a job driving a team of horses. I will never forget his words to me at that time. He was an American and came from the western part of the United States. These were his words: "Good morning, Red," (at that time I had blazing red hair), "go in there and hook up that bay and grey" (horses), "take them down to the railway station and begin carting sand to the extern portion of the city," where gangs of men were employed mixing cement and constructing a new water line. Whilst I had driven and harnessed horses hundreds of times back in Cape Broyle, I had never harnessed or driven a team of two horses before in my life. I began the work of putting the harness on each horse, but an onlooker realized my predicament and showed me how to do this. To him I was for ever grateful. Finally I succeeded in getting both these animals hooked up to one of these collapsible wagons, taking a number of shovels on board, and headed for the railway station. Immediately it was apparent that these two horses were not properly paired. The old gray was wild, whilst the bay was slow. I took the wrong street and the gray began to take charge of me as well as the other horse. It resulted in my driving the team across the city park, over the flower beds, with several policemen following me. I escaped the police and finally arrived at the siding of the railway where several cars of sand had been placed for unloading and hauling. By now I was kind of getting accustomed to handling this unruly team, but nevertheless the foreman on that end of the job gave me a severe "bawling out" for being late in my arrival.

Driving that most unruly team of horses was the most arduous day's work I ever performed in all my life. I continued working at this job for three or four days, making several mistakes in the unloading of the sand at places where the team would get stuck in that rich prairie soil. In some cases I was compelled to dump my load in front of new residences, occupied by German immigrants in the then outskirts of this growing prairie city. Eventually, the old gray horse, which had been giving me plenty of trouble, causing the slower horse even more difficulty, slipped on the new paving on what was then known as Scarth Street in the shopping area of Regina. Both horses fell to the ground. Then a crowd gathered around. A couple of police officers had their hands full to keep the people from gathering in even greater numbers. The foreman who had given me the job came on the scene, saw the mess and immediately fired me from the job. To use his own words, he told me I was "canned," to take the horses to the barn and go and collect my time at the office. Thus ended my first job in the great "Golden West." I collected my money, which was about ten dollars, and set out looking for another job. For one day I helped to move printing machinery into a new building. When the work was completed I asked the manager for a job as a stenographer. He told me that I would have to wait several months before they were ready for business. I had to eat, so I procured a job with the pick and shovel helping to dig the trenches for the extension of the pipe line. This lasted just one half day, as it came to rain and it was impossible to work in the thick mud.

During this afternoon, in the drizzle and rain, I was walking around one of the main streets looking at the shop windows when an individual whom I had never seen before in my life spoke to me. He asked me what I was doing and I told him I was waiting for the harvest to begin, so that I could go to work on one of the many farms with threshing outfits preparing the grain for market. This man told me that he had a job in a little place called Tugaske and felt that if I went with him that I also could obtain employment. The train would be leaving the following morning, we would have to change trains at Moose Jaw, taking another train up to the "Outlook Branch" for Tugaske, which was located about forty miles northwest of Moose Jaw. I told this chap I would meet him at the train in the morning. We met as arranged and started out for this little town to take part in the great harvesting of Saskatchewan's grain crop. I had told my friend English the night before of my intentions. He decided to stay in Regina and continue with his job as a teamster for the time being at any rate. English loved horses and I could understand his attitudes. We arrived at this little town in the late afternoon. It was certainly a grain-growing centre and very few people lived in the settlement. Tugaske was a place on the railway line where several small elevators had been erected to handle the crops. There were a few general stores, a branch of the Canadian Bank of Commerce, a small hotel and a Royal Canadian Mounted policeman.

After having some food in the small hotel, we started to walk over the prairie a distance of three or four miles to where this particular farmer was located. It was after night when we arrived at his small shack. The farmer's name was George Barr, a Scotsman. They lived in this small shack where he had taken out a homestead several years previous. It was a quarter section (160 acres). In addition to the farmer and his wife, there were several young children, his brother and sister, all living in this room, which they had partitioned off with blankets or quilts during the night. Mrs. Barr, a very kindly Scottish woman, gave us some more supper and we then began talking about the work which we were to begin in a couple of days time. Looking around the place, I began to wonder where we would sleep for the night. There was nothing there to indicate any kind of bunk-house or camp. Finally, the farmer took both of us out and introduced us to the barn, the only other building on the entire farm. This was to be our place of rest for that night. He told us that he was arranging for a tent for us the following day.

After this formal introduction to the residence of a couple of hungry-looking horses which we let loose on some pasture land, both of us began pulling down some straw from the stable loft and prepared our beds in the two stable mangers. We used our suitcases as pillows. I slept soundly that night in all my clothes. When I woke early the following morning, I discovered that the hens had been roosting overhead. I was a target for their droppings. My readers can imagine the state of my clothes, particularly my coat - a beautiful suit of the best English cloth which had been specially made for me about a year before at Mark Chaplin's tailor shop on Water Street. That was my first introduction or initiation, call it what you like, to harvesting the wheat crop of Saskatchewan. Whilst I felt very grieved because of the condition of my nice suit of clothes, it was nevertheless amusing and tended to give me an idea of the many difficulties I would have to face in the future. The following day we were successful in securing some sort of an old canvas tent in which to retire at night. We used horse-blankets as bed coverings. Additional men began coming along to join us in this grain-threshing work and in a few days we were kind of settled down to the general routine which was to be our way of life for the next eight or more weeks.

All this was new to me and I really enjoyed it. It was a wonderful sight on that level prairie land to see threshing machines located in all sections, blowing out the grain straw through the blower of the separator, whilst the actual grain flowed through another pipe leading into a grain bin or being loaded directly into wagons drawn by a pair of horses to the elevators, which were located alongside the railway line in the small town of Tugaske. There were eight or ten of us chaps employed by George Barr, who had acquired a threshing machine. In addition to threshing his own crops, he had procured contracts with other farmers in the surrounding area to thresh their crops. We worked from daylight until dark. There were no union hours on the prairies. I worked at both driving a team of horses, drawing a special kind of wagon to carry sheaves of wheat, oats, barley or flax to the threshing machine, pitching it into the conveyor, which was operated by a steam engine, the steam for which was produced by the burning of straw. I also pitched wheat in the field onto these wagons. I enjoyed the work. It was healthy and invigorating. Our pay was three dollars or three dollars and half a day with food found. We ate our meals in a kind of cookhouse on wheels which would be hauled around by a team of horses as we moved from place to place. The food was anything but good. Nevertheless I was in such a good healthy condition that I could digest anything. I can never forget the porridge that was served to us in the morning, half cooked and carrying large lumps of oatmeal. At that time there was no such thing as refrigeration, and the meat which should have been kept in some cool place, was left to hang outside of the old cook shack, where it was not alone subject to the hot sun pouring down upon it, but also acted as a kind of tree or post for every dog in the neighbourhood to not only take a bite out of, but also to perform some of their natural habits on. Really, I did not mind this at that time. I looked upon such incidents as part of the rough life one had to lead in this new country now in its infant stage of development. We were working hard every day and when meal time came, it did not matter to me what kind of food was served out, I ate it anyhow.

We threshed the grain for many farmers around the Tugaske area. I became acquainted with many of these fine men and their families. A great number of them were homesteaders, who had taken out one of these 160 acre parcels under the homestead plan. They worked hard from daylight until dark. In a few isolated cases, there might be an occasional farmer who had sold his farm in the eastern part of Canada or in the midwest United States, who came to western Canada and bought his farm outright for cash. I well remember one of these old gentlemen by the name of Tom Gilmore. He had a half section (320 acres) of the finest kind of prairie land close to the railway line. I talked matters over with him as to the possibilities for a young chap like myself taking up a homestead. He was most kind and friendly towards me and gave me good advice. He explained all the obstacles one would have to contend with in the establishment of such a farm on one of these "homestead plans." I remember talking a little politics with him. I knew nothing whatever of Canadian public matters at that time but I was a great admirer of Laurier.

My readers may recall that during the autumn of 1911 there was a general election in Canada. The Liberal Party, under the leadership of that great Canadian, Sir Wilfred Laurier, went to the country on a policy or platform of "reciprocity" with the United States of America. The Conservative or Tory Party which constituted the opposition to the Laurier government was led by Sir Robert Borden. This party was opposed to "reciprocity" with America, its policy being, particularly at that period, the protection through tariff barriers of all Canadian industries against competition from manufactured commodities from outside countries but particularly from the great republic of America. The Liberal Party under Laurier, who had been prime minister of Canada for some fifteen years, went down to defeat and Borden and his colleagues took over the administration of the government of Canada. I cast my first vote in that election for the Liberal representative in that Saskatchewan riding. I felt that Laurier, whom I had heard speaking in Montreal

135

earlier that year, was the greatest of all Canadians in public life. He was also a great imperialist and a strong advocate of the building up and welding together of the various dominions and colonies which today constitute the British commonwealth of nations. Another reason for my voting for the Laurier government was that I felt personally that for Canada to prosper, expand, and develop her natural resources, she must have the closest of ties with the great United States of America. I am now more than ever convinced that my judgment at that time has been proven correct, because without the many billions of dollars of American capital invested in the development of the Dominion of Canada, she would not be the young virile nation she is today.

We worked threshing on the various farms in the Tugaske area until around the latter part of November, when the coming of the frosty weather compelled us to abandon the job for the season. At this point, I cannot but express great praise for our boss and employer, Mr. George Barr. He treated all of us kindly and considerately. He was a great worker himself and was building up the farm which he had homesteaded some few years previous. I know he was having great difficulties and at times the ordinary individual would have abandoned the venture which he had undertaken. But with that true Scottish instinct for progress born with nearly every Scotsman, George Barr was sticking it out. He was living under most difficult conditions, having many financial worries and obligations. It was men like Barr that were responsible for building up the farming industry of western Canada.

Chapter 6

Roaming In The West

I remember distinctly George Barr paying us off the money due us on a cold afternoon about the last part of November, 1911. As there was no way of spending money in any form of entertainment whilst I was working at the harvest, I had about one hundred and fifty dollars in my pocket as a result of my eight weeks' work. During the last couple of weeks working on the various farms, I was wondering where next I would go and what I would do. I wondered whether or not I would return east or go further west to Vancouver or Victoria in British Columbia. Amongst the men working on this threshing job I had met an individual, an American, who had wandered all over the United States and Canada. He told me that he always spent the winters in warm climates and that it was his intention to beat his way west and south towards California. He told me he never paid any railway fares, that he used to beat his way on freight and passenger trains. He used the expression, which I never forgot, that all these railway companies had more money than he had, so why enrich them further. I then made up my mind to go to British Columbia and try my luck in beating the C.P.R.

I remember we walked in over the prairie that afternoon payday in November, to the little town of Tugaske. We caught a train to Moose Jaw where we stayed for that night in a very cheap hotel. The following morning I went down to the railway station and expressed all my luggage to Vancouver, retaining what I stood up in, which were warm and comfortable. The temperature was well below zero. Whilst I was checking, or expressing, my luggage my hobo friend, I suppose I should call him, went around the railway yard and ascertained what time, late in the evening, there would be a freight train leaving Moose Jaw going west. He discovered there would be a train pulling out around eight or nine that night and we both decided to try our luck, my first experience at this kind of travelling. We rode the top of boxcars that night as far

as Swift Current in Saskatchewan, a distance of around
one hundred and twenty miles. We jumped off the train
of cars as she was approaching this divisional point at a
very slow speed and made for a restaurant to get
something to eat. That same evening we caught
another train as far as Medicine Hat in Alberta, and the
following day we made better headway, speeding over
two divisions of railway as far as Calgary, which was
then the largest and probably the most important city
in Alberta. I left my hobo friend there, as I did not have
the nerve to try my luck beating trains through those
long tunnels in the Rocky Mountains, so I purchased a
first class ticket from Calgary to Vancouver where I
arrived one morning. I was now all alone. I registered
at a cheap hotel which cost about two dollars daily for a
room. Immediately after having a bath and change of
clothes, as my trunk had already arrived, I went to the
barber to get a clean up. I contracted certain little
animals in my head during that fall harvesting and,
thanks to that barber, I was soon rid of that most an-
noying and irritable feeling which one has when
aflicted by such insects. My readers can imagine what
it would feel like, particularly those who have had
experience on active service in the army during the
First World War.

My cash capital was now down to around eighty or a
hundred dollars and the prospects were not too bright. I
decided to go across to the island of Vancouver and see
what I could find in Victoria, the capital city of the
province of British Columbia. I was fortunate in having
an aunt, my father's youngest sister, married in Victoria. She had been married for some years to Joseph
Williams of Bay Bulls, who at one time was skipper of a
fishing banker operated by my father out of Cape
Broyle. Aunt Sis was a wonderfully religious person.
When I arrived in Victoria I got in touch with her and
lived with herself and her husband for about two
months. She had one son, Edward, who was very young
at that time. I last saw them in 1912, although Aunt Sis
came back to Newfoundland for a short visit during the
First World War, when I was overseas. Her and her
husband conducted a small grocery business on the

outskirts of Victoria. I am more than grateful to her and her husband for their kindness to me during the short period I lived with them.

A day or so after arriving in Victoria, I got in touch with Mr. M.F. Carroll, who was working in a very responsible position with Dr. Rismuller in the whaling company. He took me to see the doctor who, as I have already related, had lived in Newfoundland and had been interested with Harvey & Company in the whaling business. Dr. Rismuller's interest lay at first in the manufacture of fertilizer from the carcass of the whales. He and a Captain Balcom had established a whaling company on the Pacific coast and had made a great success of their venture. They had sold out their interests to another group, but still retained the management of the company.

Dr. Rismuller was charmed to see me and introduced me to his partner, Captain Balcom. I was invited to dinner to the doctor's home and between himself and my old friend, Dickie Carrol, I obtained a job as bookkeeper on the largest whale factory they had, located at Naden Harbour on Queen Charlotte Islands. This job was to become effective about the last of March or the early part of April, 1912. In the meantime, I worked at various kinds of jobs, such as longshore work on the C.P.R. docks, and checking freight at the same place. Yes, and I also carried the "hod," which is the hardest kind of work. Carrying the "hod" meant that I had to carry a load of some fifteen chimney bricks on my back to the mason who would be building chimneys in new homes or other buildings. The pay for this work at that time was $3.50 per day. I can assure you I earned that money and as I was strong and vigorous after my two months working arduously at the prairie harvest I was able to handle the job with efficiency.

I liked living in the city of Victoria. It was beautiful at that time; the climate was wonderful, not too warm or too cold. It was more of a residential city than a commercial city. Many people said that it was the home of retired British military officers as well as remittance men from the old country. At that time there was a small naval base at Esquimault, which is part of Victoria City. It was the headquarters of the British Columbia provincial government and the Canadian Pacific Railway had large docks as well as one of the most modern hotels of the time called the Empress. The C.P.R. operated first class passenger boats between Vancouver and Seattle to Victoria. One of these ships was under the command of Captain Patrick Hickey, who came from Torbay and had at one time been fishing on the Newfoundland Grand Banks. It was said at that time, that Hickey always operated his ship, *The Princess Victoria*, on time, and that no fog or storm prevented him from making his scheduled runs. He was a typical Newfoundlander. I remember times during the winter of 1912 when the fog was as thick as mud, but Hickey always docked his ship on schedule.

Finally the day came for me to leave Victoria by one of the C.P.R. boats for Prince Rupert, a distance of five or six hundred miles north of Vancouver. The ship on which I took passage was a beautiful vessel carrying passengers and freight. Many of the passengers were tourists, others were on their way to northern British Columbia and the Yukon territory where they were engaged in mining prospecting during the summer. It was a wonderful trip. All the way up the British Columbia coast between Vancouver Island and the mainland we were close to land on both sides. The scenery was magnificent and it was more than interesting going through the Seymour Narrows. The mountains and hills on both the mainland and Vancouver Island looked majestic and even at that time there was considerable talk of bridging at this particular point between the mainland of Canada and the island of Vancouver. I believe it took us almost two days to steam to Prince Rupert, a wonderful harbour, and headquarters at that time for a considerable fishing industry, both in halibut and salmon. I took another small steamboat that same afternoon and arrived at Naden Harbour in the northern part of the Queen Charlotte Islands that evening. I was now over five thousand miles away from Newfoundland.

Immediately I arrived at Naden Harbour and landed

on the long wharf owned by the whaling company, I reported to Mr. S.C. Ruck, who was manager of the plant. Ruck had been in Newfoundland before he went to British Columbia, had been manager of the Rose-au-Rue whale factory and had married a Newfoundland woman. He was an Englishman and, I must say, was highly competent in his position. He knew the whaling business, particularly the manufacturing end of the business, better than any other person I ever met. He had built the Naden Harbour plant for the company, which was the largest and the most modern whaling plant on the Pacific coast at that time. Mr. Ruck brought me to the office and showed me the room where I was to work, the store room which I had to take care of and the company books which had to be kept so that the records could be sent to Victoria at the end of each month. My bedroom adjoined the office. The chief engineer of the plant had a room next to mine and we had a Japanese servant to look after our various comforts. Myself and the chief engineer took our meals in a special dining room adjoining the men's cookhouse. We had a good Chinese cook and several assistants to look after the meals for the men.

There were about forty men working on the main part of that plant who had been brought out there from Newfoundland. The head oil boiler was a Newfoundlander, the chief flenser was a Newfoundlander and the general foreman was also a Newfoundlander. Several of these men came from the district of Ferryland, others from St. John's and I had known many of them before I ever thought of coming to British Columbia. Then we had about thirty or forty Japanese who worked at the fertilizer side of the plant, and were mainly employed cutting up the carcasses after the fat had been taken off the whales and then steaming the bones and carcasses in large wooden tanks to extract further oil. Also, we had around thirty or forty Chinese, who were principally employed working at the fertilizer drier. Each group, Newfoundlanders, Chinese and Japanese had their separate living and eating quarters.

From this Naden Harbour plant were operated three

and sometimes four small whaling boats. They went to sea nearly every day and there were times when we had as many as eight or ten whales alongside the slip, which had been shot by these specially experienced gunners in one day. I was friends with these gunner captains — particularly Captain Willis Balcom, a son of Captain Balcom who was a partner of Dr. Rismuller. Balcom was rated the best shot on the Pacific coast. Also, there was a Captain Anderson who came from Newfoundland and who was also a first class gunner.

The company also operated a special freighting steamer to keep its plants supplied with food and other supplies. I remember the name of this particular vessel, the *Grey*. She came to our plant every three weeks or month, and in addition to all kinds of supplies, brought the necessary cash money to pay the men. We had a general store, where all food supplies were kept, and it was part of my duty to keep an account of all food supplied the cook houses and at the end of each month send in a report to head office in Victoria as to what it cost per meal to feed the men. The food for the Japanese and Chinese was entirely separate and was shipped to the foreman Japanese or Chinese from Victoria and our company had nothing to do with this. These Orientals lived chiefly on rice and their own special kind of other foods. They were being supplied by one of the several large wholesale Japanese or Chinese companies in Victoria. At the end of each month I had to make up the payroll and pay the men the balances due them in actual cash. Then I also forwarded a copy of my cash and stock account to head office. Generally, I was kept fairly busy, as when whales were plentiful we had men working overtime and their time in hours had to be kept separately. Then the crews of the whaling steamers were paid a monthly wage and in addition they received a bonus of so much a whale. The gunners and captains of these little vessels often made as high as six thousand dollars for a season's operations.

Naden Harbour itself was a long indraft harbour, several miles in length. In one of the outside coves, there was a salmon cannery which, incidentally, was controlled financially by the same company as controlled the whaling company. The salmon fishermen were generally native Indians and had their own particular method of catching this fish. I visited this plant on one or two occasions and never saw so many salmon in my life. It was a different type salmon fish than we catch in Newfoundland, much smaller, and to me it did not have the same rich flavour as our own Newfoundland species. These Indians had their reserves in various parts of Queen Charlotte Islands, but came principally from a little Indian reserve close to Naden Harbour called Masset. The tides had an unusual drop, something like the tides around certain parts of the province of New Brunswick. At certain periods of the year, wild duck were abundant and sometimes we had a recreation period hunting these wild birds, which gave us a change in diet.

In the early summer of 1912, there was a provincial election in the province of British Columbia. We at Naden Harbour were not particularly interested. However, one day a candidate for the Liberal party, then under the leadership of Sir Richard McBride arrived at our station in a large motorboat. He had heard that there were several Newfoundlanders (British subjects) working there and even though we were not Canadians, we were British subjects, and were entitled to a vote after six months' residence in Canada. I forget this candidate's name. After he landed at the wharf he enquired for the manager and went and had an interview with him. He told Mr. Ruck that he represented the Liberal party and would like the support of the forty Newfoundlanders who were working with the company. Ruck informed this particular candidate that his bookkeeper, this young man Cashin, came from Newfoundland, that he knew all the Newfoundlanders well, that his father was a politician in Newfoundland and he advised the candidate to come and see me. As a matter of fact, Mr. Ruck introduced the gentleman to me. I then took him around and introduced him to all the Newfoundlanders and, incidentally, I was made both polling clerk and deputy returning officer. He was the only candidate that came near us and asked for our support. So, on polling day, the booth room being in our office, all the Newfoundlanders came in and voted for this Liberal candidate. It was all immaterial to us, but nevertheless, we thought that in view of the fact that he came to see us and ask for our votes, we might as well give them to him. No one else appeared anyhow.

After the provincial election was over, the sum of fifty dollars was sent to the manager, Mr. Ruck, to be paid to me. Ruck, who also had voted for this Liberal candidate, wanted to give the money to an Indian who operated a large size motor boat and had carried the ballot boxes. This resulted in a disagreement between myself and Mr. Ruck, which resulted in my resigning my position as bookkeeper, as I could not see how we could get along together in view of this particular disagreement. However, I succeeded in getting the fifty dollars and as there was a boat leaving for Prince Rupert that afternoon, I took passage by her en route to Victoria. I remember staying overnight in Prince Rupert, which town was located on the top of a hill, where one had to climb hundreds of wooden steps to get into this town. It then had a population of around five thousand people and it was expected to be the Pacific terminal of a new trans-Canada railway known as the Grand Trunk Pacific Railway. The following day I boarded another passenger boat for Vancouver and Victoria, arriving at the latter city after a couple of days. It was now around the first part of July, 1912.

Early that summer, Mr. Williams, Aunt Sis' husband, passed away rather suddenly, so the first place I went was to see where she was living and to have a talk with her. I found her and her boy living with a great friend of hers, named Mrs. Stevens. Poor Aunt Sis was not feeling very cheerful, which was understandable. Later she moved to North Vancouver, where she became a telegraph operator with the Canadian National Telegraphs. She had been a telegraph operator in Newfoundland when a young girl, and it now came in useful to her. I understand she worked with this concern for many years and was later pensioned by them. I spent a couple of hours with her and was never again to see her.

After seeing my aunt, I went to see my friend, Dickie Carrol, of the whaling company. I told him what had happened between myself and Mr. Ruck and informed him that I did not think it would be any too pleasant for either Ruck or myself if I was to remain at Naden Harbour. I did not see Dr. Rismuller as he happened to be out of town. Some years later I heard that Mr. Carroll was found on his front-door gallery, dead.

As Victoria was not a place of great commercial activity, I decided to try my luck in Vancouver. So, after saying goodbye to Aunt Sis as well as my friend Mr. Carrol, I left for this growing city of British Columbia. I was not long in finding a place where I could get a decent kind of room to live, taking my meals out at cheap restaurants. I had to conserve my cash capital, which was now around two hundred dollars. Finally, I was successful in securing a job as stenographer in the chief engineer's office of the Canadian Pacific Railway. The salary was sixty dollars per month. As I had worked for this company back in Montreal a year before, they had my record which was good. I began work almost immediately and was getting along fine for about a month. It was now around the first of August, 1912.

One night, I was going to my place of residence in a street car, when I saw, sitting just a few seats in front of me, a man whom I had known fairly well back in Newfoundland. He was a son of a well-known lawyer in St. John's, who was at that time a member of the Morris Cabinet. I was more than surprised to see any one from home. I went up and spoke to him and we got into close conversation. He had been in Vancouver for some months. I invited him to come to my room and have a talk of things in general. He left my place about midnight and we arranged to meet the following evening for supper and then to take in a show of some sort. The next evening we met as arranged, had supper and went to a show. After the show, we went to my room and had further talks, when this man, whose name I would rather not mention, informed me that he had not had anything to eat since the day before. He was broke. He had no job and told me that he was expecting some money from home. I made an appointment to meet him again the following evening and incidentally gave him five dollars out of my cash capital. The next evening we again met as arranged in a certain pool room to which there was attached a bar, where liquor was being retailed. I found my Newfoundland friend enjoying himself immensely — no doubt using the five dollars I had given him the evening before for this purpose. It kind of got me down. I had never yet taken a drink of alcohol and I could not understand why a person in his financial condition should be spending my money in this gay way of life. I had a job which was barely giving me a living and the economic condition of either British Columbia or any part of Canada was not particularly encouraging. How was I to get rid of this party who was now tailing after me? That was my problem and it was for me and for me only to find the solution. I came to the conclusion that I would best accomplish this objective by getting out of Vancouver altogether and moving east. It was now around the first part of August, 1912, just a year after I had left Montreal to find my fortune on the Canadian prairies, so before I vacated my position as stenographer with the Canadian Pacific Railway, I telegraphed George Barr of Tugaske, the farmer with whom I had worked during the previous harvest year, asking him if he would give me a job again this season (1912). My old friend George replied immediately asking me to come along. At once, I went to my boss, the chief engineer with whom I was working, and told him that I was resigning my position and that I wanted to get out of Vancouver the following night. He arranged to have me paid any balance due me by the company and I informed my Newfoundland friend that I was getting out of Vancouver and moving east on the prairies to work again at the harvesting of the 1912 grain crop. I told him how hard the work was and he seemed more than disappointed at my intention to leave Vancouver behind me, as he felt I was company for him in more ways than one. I had grown to like British Columbia, which to my mind is the finest and probably the most progressive province of all Canada at the present time. I felt sad leaving there, as I was making a few good friends, and have often wondered since what would have happened to me if I had never met that Newfoundland person in that Vancouver street car on that fine summer night in July, 1912.

Chapter 7

I Begin Moving East

On a beautiful August night in 1912, I boarded one of the trans-Canada trains operated by the Canadian Pacific Railway Company on my eastward journey to Tugaske in the province of Saskatchewan. I did not purchase any railway ticket, but took up a position in a certain part of the first-class railway car where I felt that I would be able to outwit the railway conductor or brakeman. My Newfoundland friend was at the railway station in Vancouver to see me off. He told me that he might see me in a few days. I had innocently given him my address, but never dreamed I would see him again. I managed to beat my fare as far as Calgary and had my regular meals in the dining car. However, things were becoming a bit hot, and I was forced to purchase a ticket from Calgary to Tugaske. Nevertheless I managed to save a few much-needed dollars, which, in a way, recouped for me the money I had expended unnecessarily on my Newfoundland friend, whom I was now hoping would not bother me any more.

Arriving at Tugaske in the afternoon, I immediately walked out over the prairie to my employer of the year before, Mr. George Barr. Much to my disappointment, Barr informed me that he would not be ready to start threshing for another week, but that he was able to secure me a job with another farmer named Jack McCullough. I had heard of McCullough the year before. He was then a very progressive and ambitious young farmer, who came west from Ontario, having under cultivation some eight hundred acres of rich land and operating his own threshing outfit. In fact McCullough's organization was much more elaborate, much more efficient, whilst the living quarters for the men were certainly more comfortable than those provided by my friend George Barr. More important still, the food was real good. We had a German cook who knew his job. His cooking quarters and mess room

148

were spotlessly clean. In all, this was an ideal place to work at harvesting. I had made up my mind to remain with McCullough for the threshing season, little knowing that within a few days, unexpected things would happen which would change my plans in this respect.

I had been working with McCullough three or four days stooking up wheat, following the binder or cutting machine, when one particular afternoon I received a telegram from my Newfoundland friend, advising me that he would be arriving at Tugaske on the evening train, requesting me to meet him. Before I went to meet him, I asked McCullough if he would give this individual a job. I told him his qualifications and he (McCullough) asked me to bring him along. I drove in over the prairies to meet my Newfoundland acquaintance and brought him out to the farm where I was working. He was put to work with me and another chap the following morning stooking wheat. I showed him how to do the job, which was quite simple although it was really hard physical work. He was working with us for a few days, when one morning McCullough came out in the field and took myself and the other man aboard a wagon and drove us up to another part of his farm to stook up some forty acres of oats, leaving my Newfoundland chum all alone in the middle of a six hundred acre field to carry on work by himself. He became tired and was forced to take a rest. McCullough spotted this quickly and at dinner time informed Bob that he was not suited for this kind of work and paid him off. In other words he fired him. I kind of resented this action on McCullough's part and immediately left the job also. We returned to Tugaske and went to work with my old friend, George Barr, the following day. This Newfoundlander was given a much easier job loading wagons in the field and we continued to work until the job was finished. As I have already stated, the living conditions were not nearly as good as with McCullough's outfit, but Barr was a decent kind of fellow and we worked well together. We all knew his position and those of us who worked for him gave our best to try and help him to make the grade. Our job here lasted five or six weeks. We were earning three dollars per day and our board. When George Barr paid us off we went down to Moose Jaw with the object of trying to get another job.

Arriving at Moose Jaw in the afternoon, Bob, who now had a few dollars in his pocket, got entangled with another individual, whose tactics to my mind were anything but conducive to good behaviour. Both of them began imbibing a little too freely to suit me. It was now around the end of October, 1912, and I began looking for another job. The season not being too late, there were possibilities for harvesting work around the Broadview area about one hundred and twenty miles east of Moose Jaw. I informed this mad Newfoundlander that I was leaving for Broadview on the first train out of Moose Jaw. I left Bob and his new-found companion enjoying themselves, enriching some of the western breweries and distilleries of Scotland. Arriving at Broadview after night I procured a room in the local hotel. The following morning I contacted a farmer who was looking for some men to finish the harvesting of his crop. Much to my surprise and to the indignation of my potential employer, who comes along but Bob and his companion. They were feeling no pain, which was an expression generally used of people who have been consuming excess quantities of the "cup that cheers." They were both pugnacious, resulting in the farmer having a narrow escape from having his head split open with an empty bottle. My hopes for employment with this western grain grower were now dashed to the ground.

The following day, after persuading Bob to sever his connections with his new-found associate, both of us were successful in obtaining work with another threshing outfit, operated by an Englishman, who had been farming down in Minnesota, but had moved to Saskatchewan. He had made contracts with several other farmers to thresh their crops and in one particular place we lived on the fat of the land. Finally we came to this old Englishman's own farm to finish up his grain crop. I drove one of his teams of horses used to feed the sheaves of grain into the threshing machine, whilst my native friend worked at loading in the field. When we finished this job, having had a disagreement with our employer over working hours, we were compelled to walk over the prairies a distance of some five miles with the temperature down to twenty below zero. The food dished out to us on this final job for 1912 was the most unpalatable I have ever consumed. The old Englishman was honestly the meanest man I had ever worked for. I believe we had potatoes for every meal, and I have often wondered since how I escaped contracting diabetes or beri-beri.

Arriving at a little town located on the main line of the Canadian Pacific Railway, Bob picked up a two dollar bill on the street. I was forced to say to him in my poor humorous fashion, that this was the place for us to settle, as money could be picked up on the streets. We immediately went to the railway station and ascertained that a local passenger train would be passing through during the early night going east. Bob purchased a first class ticket and sleeper to Winnipeg. He intended to make himself comfortable for that night. I told him that I was not buying any ticket, saying, as my American hobo friend had said to me a year before, that the C.P.R. had more money than I had and why should I further enrich their coffers. I informed Bob that I would meet him at the railway station in Winnipeg in the morning. I do not propose to tell how I made that overnight passage at a cost of a couple of dollars, but it was a fact that when he stepped off the train the following morning in Winnipeg, I was there to wish him the time of the day. It had cost him some twelve or fifteen dollars to travel that distance whilst it had cost me just two dollars. I was getting even with the railway company for the manner in which they had treated us harvesters the previous year, when we were treated more like cattle than human beings. I have no doubt that there were many more of my views who had travelled in a similar manner and when the opportunity presented itself, they too, were not hesitant in returning their compliments to the great Canadian Pacific Railway Company, thus expressing their indignation towards the company for its autocratic actions towards those harvesters who had travelled on such a poorly-constituted means of transportation, contributing in maintaining the fat dividends being paid the shareholders of that company in those days.

Winnipeg at that time was the largest and probably the most important city in the western part of Canada. It was the third largest city of the entire Dominion. It was the strategic centre of the grain-growing areas of the prairie provinces, its prosperity and growth depending entirely on the success of the grain crops. It was a very modern city and Portage Avenue at that time was the widest main street I saw in any city of Canada. There were more miles of railway track in the Winnipeg railway terminals than in any other place in all Canada. This was undoubtedly necessary for the handling of the thousands of cars of grain, harvested during the months of October and September, which had to be shipped through the Winnipeg terminals to the east and, in some cases, diverted from Winnipeg down through the United States.

Arriving at Winnipeg, we enquired the whereabouts of a reasonably cheap hotel and were advised to go to the Victoria, which was located near the railway station. After registering in the usual manner, taking a double room, having a good wash and general clean-up, we ran into the person who started the first silent movie picture business in St. John's and later sold out to Mr. J.P. Kielley, operator of what was once called the Nickel Theatre and was located in the Irish Hall. I had known Mr. Trites when I was a boy going to school at St. Bonaventure's College. He also knew me as well as my Newfoundland friend, Bob. He was very kind to us, giving us an idea of how conditions generally were around Winnipeg. Mr. Trites told us of a small restaurant which was located near the hotel, where we could procure cheap meals and where a Newfoundland girl happened to be working. My friend Bob happened to know this young lady, and we immediately went around to this particular restaurant. A very nice lady came to us with the menu. I had never known her in St. John's. At first she did not recognize Bob. He then mentioned to her (Bessie) that she evidently did not remember her poor Newfoundland friends. She then recognized him immediately, and we began to talk about good old Newfoundland, nearly three thousand miles away. She told us of another Newfoundlander, who was a relative of Bob's, who was at that time working as a bartender in the Clarendon Hotel in Winnipeg. Needless to say we were treated royally by this former Newfoundland girl. Our meals for the short period we were in Winnipeg cost us very little, which was a great help.

After having an excellent breakfast, we went around to the Clarendon bar, where, sure enough, we found the other Newfoundlander, whom I had known when I was working in Bowring's office, serving behind the bar of the largest drinking saloon I had ever seen. He was more than delighted to see us. Bartenders in those days were looked upon as big shots. This was just up Bob's alley and gave him an assurance of where the next drink was coming from. As I did not indulge in what was considered the manly art of drinking at that time, I began going around the city of Winnipeg to see what could be obtained in the way of work. I met a couple of other Newfoundlanders, one of whom I had known very well back in St. John's. This gentleman was in the real estate and insurance business. He gave me the impression that things were anything but bright in this prairie metropolis. I had a few dollars in my pocket and felt safe for a month. I had hopes that something would show up and I was prepared to tackle anything that offered. Bob was enjoying himself immensely, spending considerable time at the Clarendon bar where his relative, Andrew, was always in a position to quench his thirst.

Both of us were still rooming at the Victoria Hotel. We had been there nearly a week, when finally I got a line on the possibilities of work as clerk or stenographer with my old reliable outfit, the Canadian Pacific Railway, at Fort William, Ontario, about four hundred miles east of Winnipeg. The company required several clerks down there, some trouble having arisen which caused many of its employees to walk off the job. As this was the busy season of the year with the railroad, it became necessary for the company to seek help outside the Lakehead towns. So off I moved again, this time to the east. Providence was kind to me and I was successful in obtaining a fairly good job with the C.P.R. as stenographer and correspondence clerk with the general yardmaster. It was now nearing Christmas, 1912, and this job was a most acceptable gift. In any case I did not like living around Winnipeg. Now was my moment to show my qualifications in the practical side of railroading.

Chapter 8

I Settle Down in Fort William

I remember arriving in Fort William, Ontario, from Winnipeg, together with many other men who had been engaged to work as clerks in various branches of the Canadian Pacific Railway at that place. At first we lived in sleeping cars on a special siding, taking our meals in a dining car which was attached to the sleeping cars for that purpose. This lasted for a short time, until we were able to make arrangements to get accommodations in the city itself. Certainly many of those who had been engaged by the company did not remain on their jobs very long. They were either laid off or their services dispensed with because of lack of experience or efficiency. I was assigned as stenographer to the general yardmaster, Mr. A.F. Hawkins. There was more activity in this operating branch of the railway, and the possibilities for the future were much better than in any of the other departments of the company which I had previously worked, either in Montreal or Vancouver. My Newfoundland friend did not remain long with the company. He was anxious to return to Newfoundland and availed himself of the first opportunity to achieve his ambitions in this respect. To be quite frank, this particular person was not of the calibre who could make his way roughing it in the west, in addition to which, he was homesick, and wanted to get back at that time to an easy way of living.

It was not very long after my arrival at Fort William I met an Englishman, named John Booth, who worked in the same department and with whom I lived for a year or more. We succeeded in getting a room in a private home which we shared, paying something like ten dollars per month each and having to take our meals out at cheap restaurants. At that time there were two Chinese restaurants close to the C.P.R. yard office, where one could buy a meal ticket for $4.50 which entitled you to twenty-one meals. In other words our room and board cost us about thirty dollars per month. A lot of railway men, such as conductors, brakemen, locomotive engineers and firemen, patronized these restaurants and I came to know some of these fine men personally. In fact, many of them became close friends of mine. In many ways they reminded me of our own Newfoundland people. They were keenly interested in their various jobs, were kind and hospitable. I must say that in all my wanderings around the various provinces of Canada, I never met nicer people.

During the winter of 1913 the weather was extremely cold. The temperature was very rarely above zero and on many occasions it reached as low as twenty-five degrees below zero. I had never experienced such cold weather before in my life and the wind off the lake made it even more piercing. Sometime late in January, 1913, I received news from my mother that she would be in Montreal, together with her cousin, May Furlong, at a certain time en route to Rome, Italy, and would like to see me if at all possible. I had now been working with the C.P.R., on this my third occasion, for less than three months. However, I approached my boss, Mr. A.F. Hawkins, the general yardmaster, requesting three or four days leave of absence for the purpose of going to Montreal to see my mother. I was, and still am, forever grateful to Mr. Hawkins for his kindness to me in this matter. Not only did he give me the few days leave of absence with pay, but in addition, he arranged a free railway passage on the C.P.R. for me from Fort William to Montreal and return again to Fort William. I remember arriving in Montreal early in the morning and went immediately to the Windsor Hotel, where Mother and May Furlong were staying. I spent the day with Mother. May was out with Mrs. LeBel, whom I have already mentioned in a previous chapter. They had attended school together in Newfoundland and had not seen each other for many years. The four of us had dinner together at the Windsor that same evening and I took the late night train back to Fort William. I was happy at having seen my mother and she, too, was happy at finding me well and content with my new outlook in life in the important railway centre of Fort William, which was roughly a distance of one thousand miles west of Montreal.

Returning to Fort William after this fast trip and short holiday, I settled down to work in real earnest. I liked this operating end of the railway business much better than I had liked working on either of the other two jobs which I had had with the company in Montreal and Vancouver. It seemed to me that the work was much more interesting. It was real railroading in every sense of the word. It was through the yard department that all freight trains were handled. It was part of our job to see that the freight trains were made up properly — that trains of empties, which were generally moved west, made up the proper tonnage to be hauled over an up grade for the first divisional point west of Fort William. The same applied to loaded freight cars. A train west out of Fort William generally comprised about fourteen hundred tons, whereas a train coming into Fort William from the west was in the vicinity of three thousand tons. Similarly, trains going east were made up on the basis of certain type locomotive engines pulling a scheduled tonnage. All these matters were of great interest to me, and as one grew or matured in the great operating branch of the Canadian Pacific Railway, one became more familiar with its operations and more efficient on the particular job which might be assigned to him. It was certainly interesting working out the tonnages on each car of freight, to determine the size of each train.

Fort William became more attractive to me as the months went by and the spring of 1913 came around. It was located at the head of Lake Superior, adjoining another city named Port Arthur just three miles east. In those days both these cities of somewhere around the same population were named the Twin Canadian Cities. They were connected together, not alone by the railway line, but also by the operation of an electric street car system which was operated from the west end of Fort William to the east end of Port Arthur, a distance of six or more miles. The population of each city was around twenty or twenty-five thousand people and great friendly rivalry always existed between the two communities from both a social and a commercial angle. Particularly was this rivalry evident in the field of sport. I distinctly remember the many hockey games which took place between the competing teams of Fort William and Port Arthur. Generally the Port Arthur team came out victorious, but there was very little difference between these two amateur teams. Jack Adams, who always played right wing for Fort William, later went into the professional game, playing for the Toronto team and finally became managing director of the Detroit Red Wings, a team which won the World Championship on many occasions under his leadership.

All during the winter of 1913, we were kept busy in the yard office. Busy on the investigation of any accidents which might have taken place in the Fort William terminal, busy on the compiling and dispatching of trains of freight moving both east and west. It was in the yard department that the switching of all trains entering Fort William from either the east or west was handled, and the cars sorted out and placed in their respective tracks. It was from the yard department that switchmen, both foremen and helpers, received their various instructions as to the handling of trains and the placing of cars. There were several assistant yardmasters, each of whom had his particular assignment. I remember an old gentleman named Walter Jarvis, who had charge at Westfort, Arthur Lindsay who had charge of the Puzzle, from whence trains of cars were split up and placed in various tracks to be later made up into trains moving either east or west. There was Lou Gaynor, who had charge of what was known as the East End, being actually responsible for the making up of trains for both the east and west. Then there was Harry Taylor, at Port Arthur, which place also came under the supervision of the general yardmaster at Fort William. During the busy season of the year we would use ten or more switch engines working in the yard during the day time and eight or ten working at night time.

When spring came in 1913, I saw the importance of the two cities of Fort William and Port Arthur. They were the distributing centres for the supplying of the entire portion of western Canada, particularly the prairie provinces of Manitoba, Saskatchewan and Alberta. The Canadian Pacific Railway Company had large coal docks at Fort William. All the steam coal used on the railway west of Port Arthur was transported principally from American lake ports in large lake steamers and unloaded at these coal docks, later being loaded into railway cars and moved to points as far west as Moose Jaw. In reality Fort William was the real feeding centre for the C.P.R., as well as for other commercial business. The same may be said of Port Arthur, which was the headquarters of the C.N.R., then a privately operated company. All during the summer months, trains made up, principally, of steam coal were being moved west. In addition, many lake freight and passenger ships were coming to Fort William and Port Arthur from the eastern lake ports, carrying freight and passengers, and this freight also had to be discharged in freight sheds and loaded in cars for the west. At that time there was no such thing as oil locomotives or diesel locomotives pulling freight or passenger trains. The entire railway systems of both Canada and the United States were operated by steam raised by coal and locomotive firemen had to work like Trojans to keep steam up in order to maintain the schedules laid down for the operation of both freight and passenger trains.

The summer season at Fort William and Port Arthur was very warm and the temperature very seldom went below eighty degrees. In the evenings, thanks to a breeze from the lake, it was generally cool. We had several forms of recreation, and I became secretary of the C.P.R. Fort William baseball team formed by the yard department. Another team from the company was formed by Mr. John Quinlan, of the roadmasters division. This gave us all a certain interest in sports activities of the city and games would be played between our teams and teams from Schreiber, the first divisional point west of Fort William, and other times with Port Arthur teams. All in all I grew to have a great personal liking for Fort William and made scores of friends in this thriving community. It was a real railroad town and its economy depended principally on the operation of the railway and the fact that it was the terminal of all lake shipping, carrying goods and supplies for the prairie provinces of Canada, which would be loaded on cars from the various lake ships as they arrived at Fort William.

I was still living with my English friend, John Booth. We both moved from the rooming house to an apartment house on the east end of Simpson Street which was near our work. Around the early part of September, 1913, I saw my first real rush on the railroad. The grain harvested from the prairie provinces began moving east and both Fort William and Port Arthur were hives of industry. Fort William had many large grain elevators, capable of storing millions of bushels of grain and all these elevators were located along the C.P.R. railway line. It was interesting to see the train loads of grain moving in to Westfort from the west, where it was segregated into the various railway tracks to be switched by switching engines to the consigned elevators. In addition, the elevators were loading all the grain they were capable of shipping, on board lake steamers for movement to the east in a great many cases to be transferred to ocean-going ships at the port of Montreal for shipment to Europe. This additional work meant greater activity for the yard department of the railway. It meant the employment of extra train crews and yardmen and this activity continued until late in the autumn when navigation on the Great Lakes closed, sometime around the end of November or early December.

During the year 1913 I learned with great regret that my sweet old Grandmother Mullowney had passed away in her eighty-fifth year. I had been writing her regularly ever since I left Newfoundland in the autumn of 1910, and knew even at that time that she was fading gradually. Even though she lived to a good old age and even though I knew that death comes to all of us, I felt very upset when I had a letter from my mother informing me of her demise. I had always looked upon her as not only my grandmother, but also as my mother, as she was so kind to me in my early youth. I really felt, when I left Newfoundland in the autumn of 1910, that I would never see her again. She lived, however, to see my mother return from Rome in the spring of 1913 and carry to her the blessing of His Holiness the Pope.

Also in the autumn of 1913, there was a general election in Newfoundland. Again the People's Party, under the continued leadership of Sir Edward Morris, was returned to office with a slightly reduced majority. This was the election which witnessed the advent into the political life of Newfoundland of the Fishermen's Protective Union (F.P.U.), under the leadership of William F. Coaker. This union had been formed by Mr. Coaker, who had been a telegraph operator a few years before 1913, and, in my opinion, if the organization had been kept out of politics, would have been a great benefit to the people of the northern part of the island. It was in the northern section of the island that Coaker had organized, that is from Trinity Bay on the southern end to St. Barbe on the northern end. His union came out under the leadership of Sir Robert Bond, who, himself, represented the district of Twillingate. Some eleven or twelve representatives of the Bond party were elected and formed the opposition to the Morris government. Later, Sir Robert Bond became so disgusted with the tactics and policies of the Coaker union that he resigned from public life and retired to his estate at Whitbourne. In my opinion, it was a sorry day for Newfoundland when the Coaker organization entered the political field and later, as I will show, dominated some of the future governments of Newfoundland. The union went into business and established a large premises at Port Union, near Catalina, built up out of the money subscribed by the northern fishermen, who had been led to believe by Coaker that the Water Street merchants were literally robbing the fishermen, and that, by the creation of this new business organization, known as the Fishermen's Union Trading Company, the so-called Water Street merchants would be put out of business and that "grass would be made to grow on Water Street." Water Street,

St. John's, is the centre of most of the commercial activities of Newfoundland. It could be termed the "Wall Street of Newfoundland." Whilst the advent of the so-called Coaker party, dressed up in union sweaters, appealed to the innocent, simple and uninformed people of the north, the election of some eleven of its members did not in any way hamper the policies of the Morris government. It merely reduced the Morris majority by a couple of members. Later, the fishermen of the north realized that Coaker was merely using them to forward his own personal ambitions, politically and financially, and like all dictators, Coaker's power came to an end as will be described in some following chapters of this book. Father was again sworn in as Minister of Finance and Customs, an office he had held with the Morris government during its previous four and a half years of tenure. Whilst I was naturally proud that the Morris party had won the election and that the Honourable M.P. Cashin had again been sworn in as Minister of Finance, I was not particularly interested at that time in the political life of Newfoundland. All my ambitions were directed towards personal advancement in the great Canadian Pacific Railway Company.

I had now spent my second Christmas at Fort William. We of the yard office staff worked day and night shifts for seven days of the week. One of us would have every second Sunday free. I can truthfully say there was no such thing as loafing on the job. Everyone in the department was particularly interested in performing his job efficiently. Personally, I was making good progress, had received promotion and a raise of salary. I believe I became very good at the routine railway correspondence and Mr. Hawkins had become confident of my capabilities. I now felt that I was really on the road to a railway career.

The winter of 1914 was a very busy season. We were kept going hauling grain and cattle east over the railway. Considerable quantities of the various kinds of grain were being shipped to the United States. At the same time grain still continued to flow in from the west to Fort William. I had never seen such large freight trains. In many cases double-header engines pulled as many as seventy or eighty cars of grain from the western division into Fort William. Early in 1914, in addition to my regular duties of stenographer and correspondence clerk for Mr. A.F. Hawkins, I was given further promotion and made assistant chief clerk, acting as chief clerk on Sundays, at times, and night chief clerk on other occasions. I felt I was getting somewhere and was making headway in the railway business. As usual, the winter of 1914 was extremely cold. In real frosty weather, it was always necessary to reduce the number of cars and tonnage of freight to be hauled by the different classes of locomotive engines. This was caused by what is known as a frosty rail or a slippery rail. I often wondered how the switchmen and brakemen could work in the yards with such extraordinarily cold temperatures. I had never felt such severe frost in Newfoundland.

Our superintendent at Fort William was Mr. R.C. Morgan. His son, Jack, worked with us in the yard office. I became very friendly with Mr. Morgan and when he required information, at any time, with respect to the movement of special cars of freight, generally called "red car freight," he generally asked me to have them looked up. Our car record system was, in my opinion, fool proof. There were thousands of empty and loaded cars moving in and out of Fort William weekly and we could tell in a moment the movement of any car which ever went through the terminal. These records were compiled by a couple of fine young girls. I remember one of them distinctly. Her name was Tillie Carson, and she later married a railway conductor from Schreiber named Anson Mc-Cuaig. All the McCuaigs were railway conductors or brakemen, running from Schreiber into Fort William and returning again to Schreiber, which was their headquarters. Our chief dispatching office for the western division was at Kenora, which terminal was then under the supervision of Mr. W.A. Mather, who later retired from the presidency of the entire Canadian Pacific Railway system. Our general manager was located at Winnipeg, as also' was our general superintendent, Mr. D.C. Coleman, who also served as president of the company. The vice-president in charge of all western lines was, at that time, Mr. George Bury, later Sir George Bury. All these men were first class railroaders. They had worked their way up the ladder to the high official positions they held with the company. They took special pride in operating their trains on time; and if by some circumstance or other a passenger train was delayed, they demanded an explanation in detail as to why such trains were not running on schedule. In this respect it did not matter whether the delay was two minutes or two hours, an investigation had to be made and a satisfactory explanation had to be given. At that time, and undoubtedly the same system prevails in the company today, there was a merit and demerit mark system. Should any individual be found responsible for the delay in the handling of trains, or found responsible for an accident, either fatal or otherwise, he was given a certain number of demerit marks, based on the judgment of the general manager as to the seriousness of the error committed. On the other hand, if an employee did something which would be in the best interests of the company he would receive merit marks accordingly.

The summer of 1914 came around and as usual, the various shipping concerns began their season's operations to and from the head of the Great Lakes. Again, large quantities of coal had to be carried by boat, usually from American lake ports to Fort William as well as to Port Arthur. Commercial coal for domestic purposes was also handled in this manner. I had now become really interested in this branch of railway work. It was through the yard office where I worked and had now been promoted to assistant chief clerk, that all the railway train crews were notified of the times their trains would depart for both the east and the west. The calling of these various crews for their various trains was done by young call boys. These boys were introduced by the assistant yardmaster to call these train crews in their respective turns for trains destined either east or west. The assistant yardmaster had given these boys the time which each train would leave. Also attached to the yard office was a branch of the east and west dispatching office, where a telegraph operator was always on duty. The chief dispatcher at either Kenora or Schreiber was the individual who controlled the movement of all trains. The chief dispatcher at Kenora was at that time J.J. Horne and at Schreiber, the eastern division was under the direction of J.H. Boyle.

The summer of 1914 was, as usual, warm. I distinctly remember August 4th of that year, when Great Britain declared war on Germany. Those of us who remember that memorable day recall that the general concensus was that this was would be over in six months. None of us realized then that some of us would take an active part in what turned out to be the most bloody conflict in all history, involving nearly all the nations of the world; and that before this conflict ended, millions of precious lives would be sacrificed, and that ultimately, through the intervention of the great American nation on the side of the Allies in early 1917, the tide would eventually turn and that Germany would be finally beaten to her knees. None of us realized the great strength of the German war machine, which, under the domination and leadership of Kaiser Wilhelm, had been planning for years to control the destiny of the world. I remember that evening of August 4th, 1914, when hundreds of the Fort William people congregated in front of the *Times-Journal* publishing office to get the news; and how, when war was ultimately declared by Great Britain, the people cheered; and then later, how many of the friends I had made during the previous two years, who had been in either the reserve army or navy, were called to the colours. Many of them I never saw again.

I had now moved my place of residence from the apartment on Simpson Street to live with Mrs. Carter, wife of Mr. George Carter, chief clerk in the office of the superintendent. Through my work in the yard office, as well as through my association with the C.P.R. baseball club, I became a close friend of Jack Hall, the new station agent. Jack had been transferred from

Winnipeg, where he had been private secretary to Mr. Grant Hall, at that time general manager of western lines. We both took our meals as well as roomed with Mrs. Carter. It was much more home-like. We did not have to go out to cheap restaurants, which by this time, I was coming to dislike. Eating in this kind of restaurant is not too pleasant and the food did not have that "homey taste."

During the summer of 1914, my friend and boss, A.F. Hawkins, had made some changes, and I was given the temporary position of assistant yardmaster at Port Arthur. This work, which took me on the outside considerably, gave me additional experience in the operating and handling of trains in the yards. I liked this change of work. It gave me more practical experience in the railroad business. I still continued to live in Fort William and went to my work every day by street car. Port Arthur, from a scenic point of view, was a much more beautiful place than Fort William. In fact the people of Port Arthur were much more "snooty" than the people of Fort William. The city was built on the side of a hill which overlooked Lake Superior, and this fact gave the place a splendid view of all ships moving to and from the head of the lakes. About this time the McKenzie and Mann interests were constructing a railway line into Port Arthur and the Canadian Pacific handled considerable traffic of construction material for this new railway line. In addition, there was a repair dock at Port Arthur which added to its importance from a shipping standpoint. However, the real railroad centre was at Fort William, the headquarters of the C.P.R., which was in fact the controlling factor in the livelihood of almost its entire population.

Around September, 1914, my old friend and boss, Mr. Hawkins, was transferred to Medicine Hat, Alberta, as trainmaster in that territory. This was a much-merited promotion. He was succeeded by Mr. Arthur Lindsay, who was the senior assistant yardmaster. Lindsay, from a practical angle, knew more about the actual handling of trains and the yard generally, but he lacked in executive qualifications, which Hawkins certainly possessed. I was shortly moved back to Fort William from my relief job at Port Arthur and did most of Mr. Lindsay's correspondence. During the month of October, 1914, I received some holidays, and my former boss, Mr. A.F. Hawkins, extended an invitation to me to spend a few days with him at Medicine Hat. I stayed there for several days and was amazed at the natural gas which supplied this particular part of Alberta with both heat and light. In fact, the people of Medicine Hat, which had at that time a population of around ten thousand, kept their lights burning nearly all the time. It cost them practically nothing each month in comparison to what people had to pay for heat and light in the eastern part of Canada.

To give an idea of how small the world really is, I well remember one morning, after leaving Winnipeg the previous night on a west-bound passenger train, that I saw a gentleman in the observation car whom I felt certain I knew. He did not recognize me. Arriving at Moose Jaw, Saskatchewan, where we had a stop of some twenty minutes to change engines, etc., this particular individual was walking up and down the platform. I approached him and asked him if he was not Mr. H.D. Reid. He told me he was and enquired who I was. When I told him that I was Peter Cashin, he asked me was I M.P.'s son. We talked a little about Newfoundland. Mr. Reid told me that he and a couple of his friends were making a trip to the Pacific coast. When the train pulled out of Moose Jaw, I saw no more of Mr. Reid, as he had obligations which were, undoubtedly, of more interest and attraction to him than talking with me.

After returning to Fort William, having spent a most enjoyable visit with Mr. Hawkins, I again resumed work as night chief clerk in the yard department. This was not a very pleasant job. We began work at 7 p.m. and stayed on the job until seven the next morning, with a short intermission for lunch around midnight. It was in the autumn of the year and we were operating many trains of grain in and out of the Fort William terminal. Really, I did not like night work, but as it was all in the routine of trying to learn all I could about railroad operations, I felt perfectly satisfied that I was accomplishing something in this respect, and I was doing my work to the entire satisfaction of my senior officers.

It now became apparent that the war, which a lot of people had originally predicted would be over in six months, would be prolonged indefinitely. In fact, Lord Kitchener had already stated that the conflict would not be ended for four years. The situation looked grim. The small British army, called the Old Contemptibles, under the command of Field Marshal Sir John French had been driven back from Mons in Belgium. If it had not been for the indomitable courage and superb discipline of this brave little army, together with its high efficiency in musketry training, there is no question but the entire force would have been driven into the English Channel. Then, again, the French armies had been suffering heavy defeats and at one period the German hordes were practically at the gates of Paris, but providence intervened and the enemy were driven back to the river Marne. The first Canadian battalion had gone into action in France. This particular unit, known as the Princess Patricia Canadian Light Infantry, was formed by a Canadian millionaire named Hamilton Gault. It consisted principally of men who had had previous army experience and many of its ranks had taken part in the South African war. The first Canadian Division which had been in training in England was getting ready to move to France for the purpose of reinforcing the original British army and the Canadian nation was becoming more war-conscious and a general recruiting campaign was inaugurated. The statesmen of Great Britain particularly, and of Canada in a much smaller way, had wakened up to the seriousness of the danger which confronted the civilized world. The only consolation the people generally could get from the British leaders were the words uttered by Herbert Asquith, Prime Minister of England, "Wait and see."

Chapter 9

I Join The Army And Go Overseas

The winter of 1915 came around and the usual shipment of freight, both from the east and the west, continued. In fact, because of the economic effect which the Great War had on the economy of Canada, business generally was beginning to improve and prices obtainable for food commodities began to rise sharply. Western Canada, being considered the bread basket of the British Empire, supplied grain and live stock to be shipped to Great Britain. Thus, business on the railway increased and our work in the yard department increased accordingly. However, during the early winter, all young eligible men were considering joining the forces with the object of contributing to the quick defeat of the common enemy. Recruiting for the Canadian army was stepped up and the Canadian Pacific Railway company, which at that time was controlled financially in Great Britain, led the way in its patriotic effort, by agreeing to pay any of its permanent employees for six months at full salary with an assurance of re-employment when the conflict would end. This period was later increased to nine months. My salary at that time was one hundred and twenty-five dollars monthly.

I was just about twenty-five years old, and joining the army appealed to me as just another form of adventure. But what an adventure it turned out to be. Together with another friend of mine, I joined the branch of the Canadian Army being recruited in Fort William. Supplies of uniforms and other equipment were short, which resulted in us attending parades for infantry drill at specified times but continuing to work at our railway jobs until such time as adequate supplies of equipment would be forthcoming. As I look back now, it was amusing to us to turn up for drill in ordinary civilian clothes. The drill, which I had learned during my term at St. Bonaventure's College, from old Sergeant Cockshott, a veteran of the Crimean War, came back to me automatically, and in a few days I became proficient in the art of forming fours, left turn and quick march.

After being sworn into the Canadian Army, I immediately wrote home to my parents in Newfoundland informing them that I had enlisted in the forces. A letter at that time would take at least a week to reach St. John's from Fort William, a distance of around twenty-five hundred miles. After being in the ranks of the Army of Volunteers in Fort William for a couple of weeks, I received a telegram from Father, suggesting that I return to Newfoundland and join the Newfoundland Regiment. It took me a few days going through the regular army red tape to get released from the Canadian forces. The First Canadian Division had now crossed the English Channel and had landed on French soil, taking up its position alongside the regular British Army. Early in the spring of 1915 the Canadians were attacked in great force by the enemy and gas was used for the first time by the Germans, resulting in enormous casualties to the First Canadian Division. In addition, the rifles supplied the Canadian Army were absolutely unsuited for war purposes and there were instances when Canadian soldiers threw away their Canadian-manufactured Ross rifles and picked up the good old reliable Lee Enfield British rifle from a wounded or dead British soldier, in order to carry on. This particular battle was termed the second battle of Ypres and the cloth hall of Ypres will be for ever a monument to the bravery of the Canadian soldier.

Mr. Morgan, the superintendent of the railway at Fort William, was kind enough to arrange free transportation for me back to St. John's, Newfoundland, and I left by the regular trans-Canada train the first opportunity after my release from the Canadian volunteers. Many of my co-workers came to the railway station to see me off on this new but perilous adventure. To me, at that time, in my own subconscious mind, it would only be another experience in the battle of life, and several of those who said good-bye to me on the platform of Fort William Station on that memorable night, I was never to see again. They later had paid the supreme sacrifice. They joined, with other Canadians, to reinforce the First Division of Infantry which had excelled itself at Ypres, and not only was this First Division reinforced, but by the time war ended in 1918, three other infantry divisions were fighting in France and Flanders. Arriving at North Sydney, I boarded the *Kyle* for Port-aux-Basques, thence to St. John's on our own Newfoundland Railway, operated at that time by the Reid Newfoundland Company. After my experience at railroading out of Fort William, our Newfoundland system seemed obsolete, just a narrow gauge built with fifty pound steel. Our train pulled into the St. John's station on a Sunday morning during the latter part of March, where I was met by Father and Mother. I had now been away from Newfoundland for nearly four and a half years, but there was very little change in the old place. The family was now living on Queen's Road, and whilst the Cashin business was still operating at Cape Broyle, both Father and Mother spent a lot of time in the city, whilst Larry carried on the Cape Broyle enterprise.

The following Monday morning, I went up to the C.L.B. Armoury and enlisted with the Newfoundland Regiment as a private. The recruiting depot was then under the command of Lieutenant Colonel Alexander Montgomerie, who was the manager of the Furness Withy Company at St. John's. The late Dr. Paterson was the Chief Medical Officer and he and Dr. Burden gave me the necessary medical examination which I passed with ease. I felt in good physical condition and had just passed my twenty-fifth birthday. I was assigned to "F" Company. "E" Company had been fully recruited and had left for the United Kingdom. The first four companies had been training in England and Scotland. This number of infantry companies constituted a full battalion, whilst "E" Company and the eventual forming of "F" Company would be used as reinforcements for the original four companies. The first two companies, familiarly named The First Five

Hundred, had left for England on the *Florizel,* at the same time as the First Canadian Division went overseas in October, 1914.

I was issued with the usual private's uniform and kit bag and began training the following day. Additional commissioned officers had been appointed from the ranks of the First Five Hundred, returning to Newfoundland to help train us new recruits. These new officers were young, having been commissioned as second lieutenants. I remember Grant Paterson, Fred Mellor, Rupert Bartlett and Dick Shortall. Fred Mellor was our platoon commander. The company commander of this newly formed unit also returned from the United Kingdom, in the person of Captain Joe Nunns, who later died in England. Of the four platoon commanders, only one, Grant Paterson, who died in St. John's in 1976, survived the conflict. The other three made the supreme sacrifice.

It was not very long before this newly-formed unit, comprised of four platoons of infantry, was recruited up to full strength, altogether some two hundred and fifty men and officers. We received our section and platoon drill from two instructors, Jerry O'Grady and Matty Noseworthy. Both of these fine men had long experience training and drilling young men in the Catholic Cadet Corps and the Church Lads Brigade. The daily rate of pay of a private soldier in the Newfoundland Regiment was one dollar and ten cents per day, the same as in the Canadian forces. The British soldier received one shilling (24c) per day. In comparison we were millionaires.

After a few weeks of training in section and platoon drill, I was made a full corporal and received my two stripes. I was now on my way to advancement in the Army. During our short stay in St. John's, we did regular patrol duty at night time. On the nights of pay days, we had two patrols parading in the city and, at times, had to handle some difficult situations, when occasionally the boys would whoop it up. The pubs were wide open at that time. The evils of Prohibition had not yet been enforced in St. John's. When on patrol we were equipped with belts and bayonets for use in case of absolute emergency. I remember being on patrol one night and coming off duty about ten p.m. returning to our residence on Queen's Road. The late Father Veriker, the parish priest of Ferryland, was at the house. He was one of the greatest friends the Cashin family ever had. He was a real Irishman. He was an athlete in his younger days. Seeing the bayonet in my belt, he immediately took it out of the scabbard and began to demonstrate to myself and Father, how Michael O'Leary, an Irishman, had won the first Victoria Cross in the first Great War. Father Veriker did a real bayonet charge over the chairs and furniture, much to the amusement of both myself and father. He was proud of O'Leary. After a period of about five minutes, that grand old gentleman, the most saintly man I ever knew, sat down, leaving a mass of furniture upset, broken and strewn around the dining room and living room of 34 Queen's Road, much to the annoyance of my mother, who arrived to witness the final on-slaught of dear old Father Veriker on the imaginary German trenches. Really, I never saw father laugh so heartily in all his life.

Then we were advised that we would soon be leaving for overseas and all of us were given a few days' leave of absence. I remember going to Cape Broyle to visit my old friends there. As formerly, father came to Cape Broyle for the weekends, but, being Minister of Finance of the country, which now had involved itself in the war, he was generally occupied with his important ministerial office, as meetings of various government committees dealing with Newfoundland's war effort demanded his presence in the city continuously. During my few days' leave of absence, I also visited my Uncle Louis Mullowney at Witless Bay, meeting numbers of my old friends from childhood days. However, Witless Bay was not the same to me now, as my Grandmother Mullowney, whose memory still remained in my young mind, was not there any longer.

I had been away from the district of Ferryland for over four years. The only change I saw in the con-stituency was that the branch railway had been built and was operating. It was a much more convenient method of transportation for the people, but as a railroad, I looked upon it as a joke. It was poorly built. The roadbed was not properly ballasted and in comparison to any branch line of railway I had seen in Canada, it was merely a Tonnerville Trolley. Nevertheless, it served the needs of the people at that time. It had cost the treasury of Newfoundland something like a million and a half dollars, which amount, if it had been expended at that time on the construction and improvement of the main highroad from St. John's to Trepassey, would have been of greater ultimate benefit to the people. But, unfortunately, at that time, neither public men nor the people themselves visualized the phenomenal use of motor vehicles which prevails today. I do not believe there were ten motor cars in all of Newfoundland at that time. Forty years ago, if any person had predicted we would have around twelve thousand motor vehicles in St. John's alone, he would have been considered a fit patient for the mental hospital.

A few days after my return to St. John's from this short but enjoyable visit to Cape Broyle and Witless Bay, the steamer *Calgarian* which was to take us to the United Kingdom, arrived in St. John's. This ship was the largest vessel which had ever entered the harbour up to that time, having a registered tonnage of something like twenty thousand tons. She anchored in the stream to await orders. The next thing we knew we were instructed to have our kit bags packed at a certain time and, under the command of Captain Joe Nunns and the other four platoon officers, we marched with our bags and baggage to the Queen's Wharf from whence we boarded the *Calgarian* to await orders from higher authorities as to when we would sail. Finally we steamed out through St. John's Harbour. Many of those two hundred and fifty fine young Newfoundlanders were destined never to see Newfoundland again. Others of us did not return until the spring and summer of 1919. It was now April, 1915.

About this time, to synchronize with our leaving for the United Kingdom, four American submarines manned by British crews, arrived in St. John's. These underwater vessels had been purchased by Great Britain, as the British naval forces were short of such fighting craft. Our transport ship, which was armed with several six inch guns crewed by British naval officers and men, was to convoy these submarines to the great naval base in Gibraltar. One of these submarines broke down in mid-Atlantic and our ship had to take her in tow for the balance of the voyage. The fact that our vessel had to keep in sight of and in contact with these underwater craft during the entire voyage had reduced our speed to somewhere about ten knots per hour, although the *Calgarian* was capable of steaming at twenty knots per hour. All during the ten or more days it took us to get to Gibraltar we had daily parades on deck for the purpose of the usual military inspection. The water was smooth and very few of our men suffered from sea-sickness.

Before leaving St. John's, my father had invited an old gentleman named Mr. Thomas G. Morey to dinner one day, for the purpose of giving me an idea of the many temptations which soldiers in the army had to contend with. Mr. Morey particularly stressed the temptation a soldier confronts respecting the use of alcohol. He had taken part in the Riel Rebellion in western Canada and was in the ranks of the Canadian volunteer force which captured the rebel leader. Mr. Morey was a real old gentleman, and Father would emphasize the statements or information which Mr. Morey was trying to impart to me. I do not think now that I took this particular interview among the three of us very seriously. I had never taken a drink of alcohol in my life up to that time, despite all the wanderings and associations I had experienced in western Canada. Nevertheless, I admired the sincerity which lay behind Mr. Morey's advice. He was certainly a noble character. He was a great personal friend of my father. I have often thought since that time, what a shame it was that I did not take his sincere advice more to heart. At the time it was just in one ear and out the other.

We finally arrived at the great British fortress of Gibraltar, situated at the mouth of the Mediterranean Sea. From its high, rugged, rock-bound cliffs there are mounted hundreds of guns of all calibres, which guard the entrance to the eastern continent. We were told that some six hundred of these guns were mounted in these excavated rock tunnels, which were manned by British gunners. We did not have the privilege of seeing any of the actual fortress. Gibraltar is purely a British naval and army base. Naturally, after ten days of a sea voyage, we were anxious to get on shore to have a look at this quaint town, located at the foot of the great rugged hills adjoining Spain. We were not permitted shore leave on the first day of arrival, although our officers were allowed to go on shore and we learned later that they had witnessed a bull fight just across the border in some part of Spain.

The second day of our stay at Gilbraltar we were granted shore leave for a few hours. We were permitted to roam around the town as we pleased, but a specific hour was laid down for us by the naval officer in command of the ship to be on board. I believe nearly all the men, including myself, headed for a pub, many of which were located in this British army and naval base. I was really excited after stepping on shore, and forgot everything Mr. Morey had told me a couple of weeks earlier about the temptations confronting a soldier in the army. I was now to take my first drink of alcoholic beverage, a thing which I have lived to regret on more than one occasion. I little thought, at that time, that my system was incapable of handling alcohol in moderation. It took me a period of nearly thirty-five years before I came to actually realize that I was an alcoholic, that I was afflicted with that dread disease of alcoholism, one of the four major maladies being suffered by men and women of the world. I remember that whilst I did not become actually intoxicated in the true sense of the word, many of our men took advantage of the opportunity given them to drink to excess, coming on board ship strongly under the influence of that liquid which is generally called John Barleycorn. Maybe the fact that I was a non-commissioned officer at the time was somewhat instrumental in keeping me within the limits of my capacity for the imbibing of the cup that cheers, or maybe in my subsconscious mind I felt that, as I was just beginning to join that great army of social drinkers, I should go into training at first by just gradually preparing myself for the handling of greater quantities of this poisonous and artificial life-saver at some future time. I remember that as we walked up the gangway to board ship we were all searched by navy men, but despite this rigid inspection many of our boys were successful in smuggling on board an additional flask of rum or whiskey to help cheer him on his way to Berlin.

After steaming through the mouth of the Straits of Gibraltar, the ship was opened up to full speed, which was somewhere around eighteen or twenty knots per hour. We were now entering the danger zone where German submarines lurked, waiting for an opportunity to destroy as much British shipping as possible, their particular object being the cutting of the supply lines to Britain and the starving of that population. The British navy, however, had command of the sea, and it was fortunate for Britain and the other members of the British Commonwealth of Nations that Winston Churchill, who had been Head of the Admiralty at the outbreak of war, was prepared for a German attack from the sea. He knew, as no other British statesman did, the policy of the German nation, and despite all criticism leveled against him for his many actions during the First World War, Great Britain owes him for his efforts at that time, a great debt of gratitude. We were steaming in a zig-zag course to avoid submarine attack, whilst, also, we were moving with all lights out and port-holes darkened at night time. Finally we arrived at Liverpool, England, where we disembarked and boarded a special train which was to take us to Stobb's Camp near Hawick in Scotland to join the other five infantry companies of the Newfoundland Regiment which were billeted in canvas tents about three or four miles outside the town of Hawick itself.

We were now to begin soldiering in real earnest. We were to be given instruction in all kinds of drill, particularly physical drill, which was under the charge of an old Scottish soldier named Sergeant McKay. Each morning for at least one hour "Slippery Joe", as he was familiarly called by the members of the Newfoundland Regiment, put us through our paces. He had been an instructor in the British Army all his life, and was a first class swordsman and boxer. McKay had the peculiar knack of being able to be tough on parade without aggravating the men. He was particularly aggressive the mornings after pay day. He knew each man's involvement with the cup that cheers and it was nothing new for him to have several of the men doubling around the parade ground for half an hour before breakfast for the purpose of making them sweat out the hangover created from the effects of the night before. I have no hesitation in saying that Sergeant Major McKay was primarily responsible for really making the Newfoundland Regiment one of the finest fighting units in the British Army. The Newfoundlander had the material in him to make a first-class soldier and McKay moulded that material into what I would call "soldier efficiency." He was a strict disciplinarian, but he had that particular knack of being able to administer discipline and make the men like it.

After a couple of months training we were now getting into soldierly condition. The original four infantry companies, now forming the First Battalion of the Newfoundland Regiment, were moved to Aldershot, the great army centre in England. They were to be made ready to take part in the landing at Gallipoli. This was during the summer of 1915. Here was the flower of the young men of Newfoundland, full of vigour, well-trained and a credit to Newfoundland. They were inspected by Lord Kitchener, who told them they were about to enter into conflict with what he termed at that time the finest soldiers in the world, the Turks. I remember that during a short leave of absence which was given me to visit my sister Mary, at that time attending school in London, I motored down with Miss May Furlong, to see the regiment just before it embarked for Cairo, in Egypt. I met many young men whom I had known in Newfoundland for years, who were enthused over the forthcoming conflict or adventure they were to embark upon. Later, after spending a short time in Cairo, the First Newfoundland Regiment was attached to the 88th Brigade of the regular 29th Division. This particular division was considered one of the finest in the entire British Army. The landing at Gallipoli, inspired and practically directed by Winston Churchill, then First Lord of the British Admiralty, proved to be a colossal failure. It resulted in Churchill being forced to resign from his high office and later taking command of an infantry battalion on active service in France. After a few months of active service on the Gallipoli Peninsula, the entire plan had to be abandoned, and having suffered severe casualties through dysentry and actual war, the Royal Newfoundland Regiment was finally given the task of fighting the rearguard action covering the retirement of the entire 29th Division on their particular front.

Returning from my holiday in London to Stobb's Camp, we were advised that the balance of the Regiment, consisting of about two infantry companies, was to move to Newton Park School in Ayr, Scotland. I had made many friends in Hawick. These Scottish people were most kind to all of us. We had the regular soldier difficulties on pay days and by now I was able to handle my liquor, as I thought, in a manly and sociable manner. The advice given me by Mr. Morey of Ferryland just before I left Newfoundland was all pushed aside. I was now a soldier in the army. I felt I knew all about the world and in particular did I think, in my own poor subconscious mind, that I could wrestle with John Barleycorn. There were times when John put my "shoulders to the mat," but invariably I came back for more. Nevertheless, I never missed my regular parades and was becoming proficient in all kinds of infantry drill. Our living quarters in Newton Park School were much more comfortable than the old tents we had just vacated at Stobb's Camp. We were not long in finding out the places of importance to go in the evenings after our regular duties. How well do I remember several of us being regular visitors of the old Station Hotel bar in Ayr. Peggy, as she was known to all of us, was always considerate in our alcoholic requirements. Ayr was a beautiful town, located on the seashore close to Prestwick, which is now one of the great airports in Europe. There was the old Tam O'Shanter pub, where Bobby Burns and his cronies passed their sociable evenings in days gone by. There were the Burns Gardens, which were beautiful. In addition, the people themselves were most hospitable to us and many fine women took unto themselves Newfoundland husbands.

Our commanding officer was Lieutenant Colonel Whitaker, who had been seconded by the War Office from an English regiment. Whitaker was one of the family identified with the publication of Whitaker's Almanac, that annual book containing almost everything of important concern to the English-speaking world. He grew to love the Newfoundlanders and came to understand our national way of living better than any other Englishman I have ever had the privilege of serving under. In short, Colonel Whitaker became a thorough Newfoundlander himself.

Sometime around the end of September, 1915, I, together with three other young non-commissioned officers, was instructed to report to Colonel Whitaker one morning at the orderly room. The colonel informed us that we were to be given the rank of second lieutenants and suggested that we make arrangements to purchase our officer's uniform without delay. The colonel had recommended us to the Newfoundland authorities for this promotion. We were each allowed fifty pounds sterling to secure our officer's equipment. I remember myself and the late Billy Grant going to Glasgow and being measured for our uniforms, also purchasing other officer's clothing and the regular Sam Brown belt as well as a .45 Colt revolver. We celebrated this occasion in great fashion. We were gazetted as second lieutenants on October 15th, 1915. I never knew that I had been recommended for a commission and I am sure that my father, who was then Minister of Finance of Newfoundland, having considerable in-fluence in the government, did not exercise any in-fluence on my behalf. I was proud that I had done this on my own merit.

A few days after receiving my commission I was given charge of some twelve or fifteen men and ordered to report to the machine gun school at St. Andrews for training and instruction in the use of the Maxim machine gun. The old Maxim machine gun was part of the general setup at that time of an infantry battalion. St. Andrews was a beautiful little town. It is noted principally for being the headquarters of golf and I understand that the rules and regulations laid down by the St. Andrews Golf Club prevail all over the world. It also has a university, which at this time was being used as a machine gun training school under the command of a Major Sworder, a regular British officer who had seen service with the famous infantry battalion, the Gordon Highlanders, during the retreat from Mons in September 1914. There must have been at least a thousand officers and men, representing every unit in the Scottish Command in training at that particular school. The course lasted a couple of months and wound up on the final day on the sand-dunes of the golf course alongside the sea with a test for efficiency. I was the proudest young officer in the entire British Army on that particular day. I was proud of Newfoundland. I was prouder still of the two-gun team under my command, when we came off winning first place in drill and efficiency for handling machine guns in the entire Scottish Command.

I lived in one of the best hotels in St. Andrews, where many other officers from various Scottish regiments also resided. I became friends with these fine fellows. We became drinking companions and we could be found in that small barroom which opened every evening before dinner and remained open until around ten at night. Oh, yes, I was on the road to success in the army. I could boast over the efficiency of my young Newfoundland section, all of whom, with one exception, came from the outports of our island and none of whom had ever seen a machine gun before. Now we were able to lick the best the Scottish Command could produce. Fifi, the Scottish bar girl, was kept busy measuring out the proverbial scotch and sodas to us young officers. Sometimes we visited the golf club and paid additional charges for the privilege of being permitted to be honorary members for our stay at St. Andrews.

After the course was finished we returned to Ayr in triumph. We were given a new Vickers machine gun to demonstrate its deadly effectiveness to the men of the reserve at Newton Park. I was now a member of the Newfoundland officers' mess, which was located up in the town of Ayr in an old private home. We slept on the floor in our sleeping bags. We had acquired a band and a fine old English bandmaster named Worthington. Our men were being reinforced regularly from Newfoundland, and around the first part of March, 1916, five or six of us young officers, as well as a couple of hundred trained infantrymen, were ordered to get ready to proceed to France to join the original Battalion which had now been transferred from Egypt to the Western Front. We were now on our way to Berlin. I am the only one of these young officers who survived. The others, my friends, my comrades, paid the supreme sacrifice and did credit to Newfoundland.

Chapter 10

We Leave For France

I well remember the evening in April, 1916, when some two hundred and fifty officers and men paraded in full marching order in front of our Newton Park barracks in Ayr, Scotland, proceeded to the small railway station near the barracks, from where we boarded a special railway train, which was to take us to Southampton in the English Channel to embark on a troop ship which was to take us to France. I will never forget that particular evening in Ayr when the command was given for quick march. We were followed by hundreds of residents of that beautiful town — people with whom we had been associating for many months, amongst whom many of us had established very close friendships. It would have been interesting if we could have had a movie picture made of that scene at the railway station. These fine Scottish people had been treating us so kindly and hospitably, that parting with them reminded me of parting with my own people in Newfoundland.

Many of the boys had been celebrating the occasion and a great number of them, including us young officers, were feeling no pain. Eventually, after a lot of difficulty, we were able to get all our men on board the train and pulled out for Southampton. The cheering by both soldiers and civilians finally died down as the train slowly pulled out of the Ayr station. We made a special stop at Newcastle that night for lunch. Colonel Whitaker had sent Ken Goodyear along with us to give us any help we might need. I am proud to be able to say that the general behaviour of all ranks was excellent.

Arriving at Southampton in the morning, we fell in the company in four platoons under the command of Lieutenant Fred Mellor. We called the roll and discovered we had one man too many. This particular chap had stowed away, having made up his mind that he was going to the Front. We gave him in charge of the

183

military police at Southampton to be returned to Newton Park, but when we fell in our parade the following morning in Rouen, France, this particular soldier was still with us. We then decided to take him along to the base depot with the company and have his military documents forwarded from the battalion headquarters in England. We proceeded in full marching order about four or five miles outside the city of Rouen to the base depot, where many other Newfoundlanders joined us who had been returned from Gallipoli to join the regiment in France. There were thousands of soldiers from nearly every unit of the British Army located at this particular base. They were reinforcements for their various regiments. It was obvious that plans for a general all-out attack were being made by the higher command and final training was being given to all ranks in preparation for the great onslaught.

We were on parade from early morning to late afternoon. We were receiving our final training for the great event. Our men were in good physical condition and we did not mind the hard grind. For eight or ten days we went through all kinds of training. In spite of these daily manoeuvres, we were able to get time off in the evening to visit the historic city of Rouen, to see the place where Joan of Arc was burned at the stake, and many other points of historic interest. The town was wide open, to use the popular phrase. The restaurants, bars and shops were doing a roaring business, and we soldiers, knowing that we were headed for battle, were having our fling.

The eventful day was not long coming around, when we entrained for the front, where we joined the regiment, a few miles behind the front line at Beaumont Hamel. I was assigned to "B" company, then under command of Captain Joe Nunns. A few days after our arrival at battalion headquarters, we took over the "front line" in front of Beaumont Hamel, from one of the British units of the 29th Imperial Division, to which our regiment was attached. Each night we were assigned patrol duties and the stringing of barbed wire entanglements. At that time everything was quiet on the entire front. Its quietness was really an indication of something brewing and all ranks were kept on their toes. This patrol duty and handling of barbed wire was both hazardous and difficult. The line was quiet, with only the occasional shell fire, nothing serious. However, one night, after returning from one of these patrol duties, after taking off my gas mask and the proverbial tin hat, I went outside our dugout for a few minutes, when one of these stray shells came over and burst right in front of me. Before I could take complete cover I was hit in the head by fragments of the shell, causing a very deep gash in my skull. I was immediately rushed down to the dressing station, where I was bandaged up by our first aid unit and sent on down the line, being admitted to the base hospital at Le Toquet. This wound, whilst not really very serious, caused me great pain, and the nurse in charge of the ward had great difficulty in preparing me for the operation I was forced to undergo in order to have the shrapnel removed from my head. This particular military hospital was located in the old gambling casino and had been known as the Duchess of Westminster Hospital, having been originally organized by the Duchess. It was an officers' hospital and several hundreds of officers of all ranks were being treated there. In fact, it was reputed to be the best military hospital in France at that time.

Having spent several weeks in this hospital I was discharged and sent over to England, where I entered No. 3 General Hospital at Wandsworth in London. This was the particular institution where most Newfoundlanders were sent after being wounded or contracting some other illness. I spent a very few days there, before I was finally discharged and was granted leave of absence for a couple of weeks. When I went to our record office in London, Major Timewell, the paymaster, informed me that Sir William McGregor, who had been Governor of Newfoundland for several years, had been looking for me. Sir William had extended an invitation for me to spend my leave at his home in a small town in the south of Scotland. I took advantage of this kind invitation and proceeded immediately by train to the country estate of Sir William.

This estate consisted of several hundred acres of farm land and forest, most of which Sir William had rented out to farmers. He lived in a large brick house which had formerly been a monastery of some sort. I spent a week or ten days here and, as the place was very quiet and Sir William ran his home on a certain plan which had to be strictly adhered to by all his family, I made up my mind to get away from this hospitable place as soon as convenient. I wanted to get out and have a good time and the kind of time I was seeking could not be had at this place which was run according to schedule and on strict disciplinary lines.

After spending a couple of weeks on general leave of absence, spending most of that time in London and Edinburgh, I returned to our base headquarters, which was still located at Newton Park in Ayr, Scotland. This would be around the first part of June, 1916, or shortly before the memorable day, July 1st, 1916. I refer to this day as memorable, because on July 1st the Newfoundland Regiment had taken part, with other units of the British Army, in an all-out attack on a very wide front along the river Somme. This was the great drive which had been in the planning stages for several months. It was preceded by an intense bombardment with all calibres of heavy and light artillery, which was concentrated on the German front and support lines. The idea was to obliterate any German defences by such bombardment, so that our troops could make a frontal attack and occupy the enemy lines. Then our artillery was to be lifted, so that the rear German trenches and general lines of communication could be destroyed by our artillery. Our general staff planning did not work out as was anticipated. The general staff had not counted on the fact that the Germans had built very deep dugouts and numerous enemy troops could be sheltered safely from our artillery fire. The result was that when our troops attacked, after the lifting of the artillery barrage, they were confronted by incessant machine gun fire all along the front. These machine guns had been placed in properly constructed shell-proof emplacements which could pour a hail of death into any attacking force. It was against such a well-protected front that the twenty-ninth Division, to which the Newfoundland Regiment was attached, had to advance. The result, of course, was that no valour, no heroism or determination of any troops could make headway, and whilst the Newfoundland Regiment covered itself with glory on that historic first of July, 1916, it was practically wiped out. Commenting on the part played by our Regiment, a few days after this particular battle engagement, Field Marshall Sir Douglas Haig said that the Newfoundland Regiment was better than the best. I think it can be truly said that the battle of the Somme, whilst some trivial advances were made, turned out a colossal failure. It did, however, show our general staff that in order to defeat the enemy or to prevent his defeating us, we had to adopt both offensive and defensive tactics, which up to this time we had completely ignored.

And so it was that the creeping artillery barrage, and the indirect overhead firing of strongly-emplaced machine gun batteries was inaugurated. The adoption of special machine gun battalions being attached to the various divisions was brought about under the sole command of special machine gun officers, trained in the tactical handling of machine guns both in attack and defence. Each machine gun battalion was under the command of a lieutenant colonel, with headquarters at divisional headquarters. The battalion consisted of four machine gun companies, equipped with sixteen Vickers machine guns, each company under the command of an officer of field rank, generally a major, and nine other officers, which included a second-in-command, generally a captain, and eight junior officers. Such a set-up had its own transport officer who had charge of ten horses and some ten mules and general service wagons to carry the guns and ammunition, as well as food rations for the troops. Each gun was capable of firing about 500 rounds of .303 ammunition per minute.

This new plan for the handling of machine guns entailed the setting up of special training schools in England for the training of machine gun units; after such training, the units would be assigned to the various infantry divisions fighting in France, Belgium and several other theatres of war. It was really a copy of what the Germans had already put into effect in their forces. Naturally, to establish such a training scheme took some considerable time before the training centre could get into actual training operations. The plan had been put into effect in France, and was working well, but these units had to have reinforcements because of casualties, whilst it had become evident to the general staff that to bring the enemy to a complete and all-out defeat, further infantry forces had to be engaged, trained and equipped before they would be fit to take their places in actual battle engagements. All this planning, training and equipping took valuable time and it would be almost a year before our active forces on the various fronts would have further support against an enemy which outnumbered us greatly. The British tactics, then, had to be to hold our own until such time as the training of infantry divisions, artillery and machine gun units could produce effective, trained personnel, who could take their places in the line of battle. This is no time for me to criticize the actions of the British staff of the 1914-18 war. There is no doubt whatever in my mind that the failure of our governments, general staffs and those responsible for the defence of our way of life prolonged the duration of the First World War by at least one year, and that thousands of lives were unnecessarily sacrificed because of such failure.

Having had three or four months practical training in the use of machine guns when the machine gun battalion idea was conceived by the British authorities, I made application through my Newfoundland commanding officer to be seconded to the Machine Gun Corps, but retaining my commission as a Newfoundland officer. It was not long before my application was given favourable consideration by the War Office and I was instructed to report for duty to the headquarters of the Machine Gun Corps, which had been established at Grantham, near Nottingham and only a few hours' train ride from London. I was assigned to an officers' section for training purposes and our billets were under canvas for sleeping quarters, whilst we took our meals in large huts specially built for the purpose. To give an idea of the officers' messes which were located at the training camp at Grantham, we had one officer's mess, where some two thousand officers of all ranks took their meals, and four bars located in this building for the sale of alcoholic beverages. One can imagine then that there were times when discipline of the army sort was difficult to enforce and it would be strange if, during the period of one week, there were no courts martial, or some officers being returned to their regiments as unfit for service in the Machine Gun Corps.

The training program was stiff. We had to start from the very beginning under charge of British non-commissioned officers, who knew their drill from beginning to end. As we progressed we would be assigned to more advanced technical training which included training in mounted drill. I regret to have to admit that my proficiency as a horseman was anything but up to standard and I was continually in difficulty with the instructors, but finally, because of the necessity of trained gunners, many of us were transferred to another camp located in Belton adjoining the training camp. I was assigned to machine gun company 178 under command of a Captain Denroche, an Irishman who had been at school in Ireland with Kevin Keegan, an officer in the Newfoundland Regiment. This would be around the month of November, 1916. The command of this particular reinforcement base was under Lieutenant Colonel Aplin, a regular British officer, who had been in charge of machine guns in an old cavalry regiment. Aplin was of the old type British officer, who looked down upon those of us who came from the colonies as ignorant colonials, most ignorant of everything and difficult to handle. He was arrogant, egotistic and intolerant. He was the type of British senior officer who delighted in having junior officers bow to his self-opinionated intellect with awe. He gloried in having people crawl at his feet.

Bolton Park was the base where several new

machine gun companies were formed under the supervision of the commanding officer and wing commanders. We trained our companies daily in co-operative tactical exercises. Every day of our short stay at this training centre was fully occupied and, honestly, I was delighted when, early in March 1917, we received orders to proceed to France and our full battalion, with all equipment, guns, ammunition, transport, horses and mules entrained at Grantham for a Channel port where we embarked on a troop ship for Calais. From Calais we proceeded towards the front line to join a British division. Our machine gun company, under command of Captain, later Major, King, was attached to the 46th British Division. Our new battalion commander was Lieutenant Colonel Basden.

Chapter 11

I Return to France and Battle

Arriving near divisional headquarters, which were located a few miles behind the front line near Loos, each machine gun company of our battalion was attached to an infantry brigade. A great number of our company had seen action before and we all had an idea of what the future held in store for us. Those who had no previous battle experience were soon to receive their baptism of fire. We had a first class company of gunners, well-trained in tactics, and before long we found ourselves in the line of actual combat.

I had been promoted to the rank of first lieutenant in October, 1916, so, being one of the senior officers in the company, was given command of a machine gun section, which was comprised of four guns, manned by some twenty-five men. I had as my sub-section commander a young sub-lieutenant from the Royal Scots Regiment named Bryce. We took up our positions opposite the German front line which ran along in front of the town of Lens. Each night we harassed the enemy with indirect overhead fire. This new system of using machine guns as sort of light artillery had been worked out mathematically from the map of the area which showed both the enemy and our own trenches. We could get good results and accurate fire at ranges up to 2900 yards.

It was now about the month of March, the trenches were wet, but we considered the line quiet. Nevertheless, we concentrated heavy machine gun fire on the enemy rear lines every night. We continued to worry the Germans with these sort of tactics. Each evening orders were received from our machine gun headquarters as to what points in the enemy lines we would concentrate our fire on for that particular night, opening fire once darkness had set in. We discovered this method of tactics must have had its effect, because invariably the enemy would reply with intermittent barrages of fire from their light artillery, generally concentrated on our front and support lines. Our gun positions were well-protected and camouflaged, so that it would be difficult for the enemy to locate and get a direct hit on any of our emplacements.

This part of the front had been the scene of many bloody battles. It was along our particular front that the historic Battle of Loos had taken place in 1915, when some of the new divisions of the Kitchener Army were thrown into action in what turned out to be a tragic failure. It was right along this front that the famous Fifty First Highland Division made such a heroic stand and by its heroic deeds gained for itself the title of the finest fighting division of the entire British Army. One would have to actually have seen what was left of the town of Loos and other French villages around this area to get an idea of what had happened. There was not one building of any sort left in this town: it had been battered to rubble by the fire of both German and British guns.

The Canadian Corps, under the command of Lieutenant General Sir Arthur Currie, held the line immediately to the south of us and on our right flank. The Canadians were planning an attack on Vimy Ridge. The ridge was being held by the enemy and commanded an excellent strategic position overlooking the town of Arras and surrounding territory. Our divisional machine guns and artillery were given the task of supporting and defending the left flank of the Canadian forces by concentrating our fire on the right flank of the German defence forces. We did this at a range of over twenty-five hundred yards. The general artillery bombardment had been progressing for several days prior to the actual attack, but on the morning of April 9th the Canadian infantry left their trenches, supported by artillery and machine gun fire, succeeding, after tough fighting, in taking Vimy Ridge and, following several days of repulsing German counter-attacks, finally consolidated their positions. This was one of the greatest achievements of the Canadian Army during the entire war of 1914-18.

We continued to hold our line along the Loos front,

being relieved for a period of a week or ten days at intervals, going back near the town of Bethune for a clean up and rest. Our rest period was a time when our men took baths, were given clean clothing and visited the neighbouring French villages for general relaxation. The French people located in these areas had wonderful courage. The occasional German heavy shell being dropped in their particular village did not worry them too much. They continued about their work on the various farms and their estaminets or restaurants were doing a roaring business with our troops. They sold the cheapest kind of wine and sometimes good meals, depending on which village or town one was located in. Occasionally, not very frequently, an enemy aircraft would drop a light bomb, and the Germans might send over a heavy shell, but, generally speaking, this particular part of the front could be considered quiet, and we did not worry too much about any heavy shelling or bombardment from the air. We were enjoying ourselves while out of the line. We visited Bethune, a mining town about seven miles from the German trenches. It had been heavily shelled during the battle of Loos, but now it was a place where soldiers went to enjoy themselves. The Canadians had established an officers' club in the town and us Imperial officers, as we were called, had all the privileges given us that any Canadian officer enjoyed. We took advantage of this and each evening four or five of us young officers dined and wined in the Canadian officers' club at Bethune. We knew we would be returning to the trenches in a few days and we were determined to make the best of it while we were out of the line. There was plenty of alcoholic beverage to cheer us along our way. This was supplied at very cheap rates by the British canteens, whilst French champagne was cheap in comparison to what we have to pay for it today. I can only remember one occasion when we went short of our liquor during all the period I was at the front.

Our division continued to hold this part of the fighting line all that summer, taking part in several engagements with the enemy. One such engagement stands out in my mind vividly today. It convinced me at that time of the value of machine guns, not alone for use in attacking enemy positions, but particularly for use in defensive action. It told me something of the actual difficulties which confronted the Royal Newfoundland Regiment when it advanced to the attack on Beaumont Hamel on July 1st, 1916.

On this occasion, around the middle of August, 1917, a division of Canadian infantry was ordered to attack the enemy holding Hill 70, located north east of the town of Lens. Our guns, which were directly behind that infantry, were ordered to give supporting fire to the Canadian troops. The Canadians, after an intensive bombardment of the enemy lines by artillery and machine guns, went over the top about 7 a.m. They took their objectives after very severe fighting and began the consolidation of their new positions. Then the enemy artillery laid down a very heavy barrage of artillery fire on our lines. We were fortunate in that we had moved our guns about fifty yards forward of our original positions during the night previous and we held on tight to our newly-formed lines. The same afternoon, following the intense bombardment of our trenches, the German infantry counterattacked with a brigade of Prussian Guard troops. They made this attack in close formation. This attack, made in close column and lead by an officer riding a white horse, presented the most beautiful target I saw during the entire war. Our guns opened fire at a range of not more than eight hundred yards. These guns were working perfectly and inside of ten minutes we had wiped out the entire attacking force. My readers can well imagine the havoc which some forty or fifty machine guns would create firing at the rate of five or six hundred rounds of .303 ammunition per minute. It was nothing more or less than a slaughter. It was this particular engagement which definitely convinced me of the advantages of machine guns in defensive warfare. It gave me a slight idea of the obstacles which our Newfoundland Regiment were confronted with in its attack on Beaumont Hamel. After a few days the Canadians had consolidated their new positions and we went out of the line for the usual rest and clean up.

The Americans had declared war on Germany and her allies in the early part of 1917. American troops were arriving in France, and some of them were even being attached to British and Canadian units for training purposes. We were holding on to our lines in conjunction with our French allies, the policy being to await the support of the American army before any further attempt would be made by us to break through with an all-out attack on the German front. Having now been continuously on active service in France for more than six months, I was granted leave to England for a period of two weeks. So, while my unit was resting behind the lines, I had the privilege of spending ten days' holiday in England and Scotland. It was good to get back again to London and Edinburgh where I enjoyed myself thoroughly and returned again, after a couple of weeks, to my company, looking forward to another period of pleasure six months hence. My company was still holding our old front in the Loos-Lens area, but we had moved our guns further forward to the old chalk pit, located very close to Lens.

In this particular part of the line we located ourselves in old German dugouts which were built by our enemy to a depth of thirty or forty feet underground. It was here that several American officers came with us for a week's instruction and we put on a special raiding attack for their benefit one afternoon. Well do I remember this particular occasion, because after the show had been pulled off most successfully, our infantry having raided the enemy trenches and captured several German prisoners, I returned to my dugout, there to discover that the American officers had been there ahead of me and helped themselves to what Scotch whiskey I had saved to celebrate the occasion. However, the rum ration which came up every evening, helped to cool off the state of nerves which one suffers after a show of this sort.

During all this time, our division formed part of the Third Army, which was under the command of General H.H.G. Byng, later the first Baron Byng of Vimy, who became Governor General of Canada. This army, made up of two or more army corps of infantry, artillery and machine guns, held the line practically all along the front of the river Somme. Considerable shifting about of divisional troops took place at intervals.

In the meantime, the British Army to the north of us, known as the First Army, had been planning an attack on the Belgium front. This particular part of the battle front had been the scene of very heavy fighting in 1914 and 1916. It was the scene of the first use of poisonous gasses by the Germans, when the first Canadian division suffered heavy casualties. It was a position subject to heavy enemy fire in the Ypres Salient, from the commanding position held by the Germans which overlooked our lines. The objective was to try and straighten out this part of the front, so that the enemy would be unable to harass our troops with enfilade fire. In addition, the planned attack was for the purpose of keeping the Germans occupied, so that further minor attacks could be made on other parts of the front. The attack which ultimately took place was anything but successful. Whilst our troops, supported by heavy artillery fire, took their first objectives, it was found that the German positions were strongly defended by artillary and machine guns, with the result that considerable casualties were suffered, which in the long run did not warrant the efforts which were made to straighten out this section of the battle front.

At the same time, plans were quietly being made by our general staff to try and break through in the Cambrai area, which was located south of our divisional front. This was one of the first times that armoured tanks were used with any degree of success. The attack was planned to take place around the first part of November, 1917. The Germans had been preparing strong defences in the form of unusually wide trenches, with deep dugouts to shelter troops and machine guns placed in strategic positions in concrete emplacements. These dugouts and emplacements were found to be practically shell-proof. When the first wave of attacking tanks moved out from carefully-concealed locations and headed for the German front line of

defence, the enemy was taken by surprise and fled for a
short time in utter disorder, but eventually, after advancing a few miles, and because of the failure of our
reserve troops to arrive on schedule, our attack was
slowed down, the German light artillery came into
action and the tanks, being very slow at manoeuvring,
just three miles per hour, made easy targets for the
German gunners. The portion of the front known as
Bourlon Wood, which had been blown to pieces by our
artillery, was a network of German machine guns
which again obstructed any possible advance by our
infantry troops. The Germans, supported by a heavy
bombardment of all-calibre guns and using mustard
gas fired from light artillery, counter-attacked and
drove our troops back to their original positions. Our
division was rushed in to support the other British units
and for a time we were practically surrounded by the
enemy, but eventually we were able to fight our way out
of the salient into which we had been forced. Finally,
after several days intense fighting and having suffered
thousands of casualties, we had to retreat from Cambrai and take up our positions from whence the attack
had originated. The battle of Cambrai was another
unsuccessful attempt to dislodge the Germans from
their strong, well-defended front.

After coming out of the line at the close of this particular battle, I found I had been promoted to the rank
of captain and was made second-in-command of
another machine gun company. I also received a
telegram from my mother, which had been forwarded
to me from the Newfoundland office in London. This
telegram conveyed to me the sad news that my brother
Dick had died. I had become accustomed or hardened
to a soldier's life and had witnessed many deaths, but to
hear of poor Dick's death saddened my heart. The last
time I had seen him was when I was returning to
Newfoundland from Fort William to join the
Newfoundland Regiment in March, 1915. At that time
Dick had been working with the Bank of Nova Scotia in
Moncton, but he had resigned his position with the bank
in the meantime and returned to work in the Cape
Broyle business. I received particulars of his tragic

passing in a further letter from Mother later that month. I am sure things would have been different in our family relations if only God had spared Dick's life. He was a great fellow and was very popular with all the people with whom he ever came in contact. He was a man's man in every respect.

The new company to which I was attached and of which I was second-in-command was located some miles from my old 178 company. Like my old company, it was a British officered unit functioning along the same lines. Whilst I was proud of the promotion, I was sad leaving my old company, because I had been in at its formation at Grantham and had lived, fought and suffered with the officers and men, to whom I had become greatly attached. Nevertheless, it was not long before I became accustomed to my new duties and was shortly to grow to have the same regard and respect for these fine fellows. The duties of second-in-command of a machine gun company at that time were not as arduous or, for that matter, as risky as the duties of a section officer or as a commanding officer. My duties were more administrative than anything else. Although I had quarters behind the front line, there was never a day whilst our company was in the trenches, that I did not visit the officers and men.

We (my new company) had taken up positions just south of Arras and our division, now the twentieth, was comprised, as usual, of all British troops. As the American forces were arriving in France now in great numbers, it undoubtedly had been decidéd to hold what we had and prepare for an all-out offensive. We followed the same routine as I had been accustomed to in my own unit. We had our systematic reliefs from the trenches, when we came out to rest in a small town close to Doullens and not far from the city of Amiens. Our rest period was usually one of cleaning up and pleasure. We generally visited the town of Doullens and partook of delicious French food. We were making up for the deficiency in our diet which sometimes we experienced in the trenches. My daily pay had now been raised by more than a dollar per day after promotion to the rank of captain and I regret to say that at that time economy was not my strong point. I think the same applied to most soldiers, officers and men alike.

My new machine gun company was still a unit of the Third British Army and the commander of my new company was a Captain Needham whom I had known previously when we were forming up the new machine gun companies at Grantham in the autumn in 1916. We continued to do our turns of duty in the front line, being relieved every ten days or two weeks, when we would come out to rest and clean up. Our rest quarters were located around Doullens and Amiens.

We were lucky when Christmas of 1917 came around and we found ourselves out of the line. Christmas in those days in France in the army was looked forward to just as if we were safe at home. Preparations were made for the great event. Special Christmas dinners were prepared for the men and the officers generally acted as waiters for the occasion. A special ration of rum was provided for the occasion and army discipline was forgotten for that day. The men's dinner was served about noon and ended late in the afternoon, with the usual speeches and toasts, etc. Then, at night, the officers held their special festivity. Turkeys had been supplied or bought for the occasion and, needless to say, in addition to the rum ration, extra liquors and wines of all kinds were purchased by the mess. Christmas of 1917 was really one of the most enjoyable I had ever spent. We relieved another machine gun company in the line December 31st, 1917, in order to give them the New Year's holiday which they enjoyed in a similar manner as we had Christmas. And so the year 1917 closed with anticipation and the hope that Christmas 1918, would find peace and happiness for the civilized world.

Chapter 12

1918 Brings Despair and Victory

We spent the first part of January, 1918, in the trenches. Our positions were a few miles south of Arras. As I was now second-in-command of the company, my duties, as already outlined, were more of an administrative character. Having some sixteen gun teams holding positions in the front line, I was responsible for seeing that they were properly supplied with food and ammunition as well as all other commodities necessary to keep the unit in sound preparation for either an attack by the enemy or an advance by our forces.

Looking back over the results of our general progress of 1917, it was anything but encouraging to find on an analysis of the various actions which took place, both offensive or defensive, that, even though our allies and our own forces had suffered enormous casualties, the only real progress which had been made was the action of the Canadian corps at Vimy Ridge. The attack by the First Army in the Ypres area of Belgium had been a failure and certainly the attack in the Cambrai area was a huge bungle and could, in a sense, be looked upon as a real defeat. Our thoughts were now concentrated on what would be the result of our 1918 activities.

The American army had been arriving in France in large numbers during the latter part of 1917. They had not been sufficiently trained, were a civilian army, really, and it took considerable time for them to get properly organized and properly trained before they were fit to take over the portion of our front in the south and give much-needed relief to the French army which had not yet recovered from the brutal battle of Verdun. The British army in the north, which included, in addition to the English and Scots, the Canadian Corps, the Australian Corps, the New Zealand Division, as well as the South Africans and Indians, were now holding fast, and orders came to build up our defences and harass the enemy with intermediate raids and nightly bursts of machine gun and artillery fire.

The Germans had built up what appeared to be a solid defence all along the front. They held the commanding positions, and it is questionable if, in any part of that long front, they did not command the most strategic and important positions. In many instances and places, the enemy commanded positions where both their machine guns and light artillery could plaster us with enfilade fire, which is most destructive. The entire German front had been built up with such thoroughness, with deep protective dugouts capable, in some cases, of sheltering an entire infantry company, with concrete machine gun emplacements all along their front and supporting lines, it appeared to us at that time that it would be next to impossible to break through those defensive positions.

We had now become aware through our intelligence corps that the Germans were contemplating a final grand assault on our whole front. They were concentrating troops in great numbers in the north and south, but it was felt that the British armies, which included the Commonwealth forces, would have to bear the brunt of the initial attack. We were now in a state of uncertainty, we continued in our same positions, being relieved every ten days and training for defence. It had now become a battle of nerves. Tension was very prevalent throughout our entire organization. Any unusual action by the enemy in the way of additional artillery fire or machine gun fire caused a flurry, and in fact, we were continuously on the alert.

This continued all during the winter. Our troops were in good shape though tension at times created a feeling of "jitters" amongst all of us. We knew, or at least we felt, that the attack by the enemy would soon come and we longed to get the thing over with. Finally, on March 21st, 1918, about 6 a.m., the Germans opened up with the most intense preliminary artillery fire of the entire war. At least it was the most intense I had ever witnessed.

We (our machine gun company) under command of Captain Needham had our sixteen machine guns in the forward area, with none in reserve. Not one of our guns came out of that action — the entire sixteen were blown to bits. When the battle dulled a little in the afternoon, we found the Germans advancing along sunken roads in many instances, in close formation and with very little opposition. We had learned another lesson — never put all your efforts in advance territory — keep a portion in reserve. That evening, out of ten officers and some 150 men, there remained only myself and the transport officer and about fifty men. The latter were amongst the drivers of the transport section. The eight officers in the line were either killed, wounded or taken prisoner. In fact, we never really heard of any of them again.

The Fifth Army (British), under General Gough, holding a very thin and lengthy line of defence on our right flank, broke, and we, without any guns and nothing but the occasional Lewis gun, heavy artillery and rifles were also forced to retire to conform with the line. We fought every foot of the way and finally, with bits of infantry, the occasional machine gun and some field artillery, together with cooks, batmen and every available individual, were able to hold a line and were successful in saving the city of Amiens from enemy occupation.

The Germans were now making their last supreme effort to cut the British Army off from the French and American armies in the south, and drive us into the Channel. By an act of providence the enemy had failed in this last outright effort to bring the British and allies to their knees. If they had succeeded in capturing Amiens, they would have cut the rail line through which all our supplies were moved from Britain. The French army had been in bad circumstances ever since Verdun and the British leaders had fumbled every effort they had made to force the retirement of the enemy. General Gough of the Fifth British Army was relieved of his command and sent back to Britain under a cloud. It was not until many years after the war that he was exonerated of all blame in connection with his forced withdrawal. He had been continuously asking for reinforcement to bolster his thin line of defence but the British high command had not heeded his requests and Gough was made the scapegoat.

It was just shortly after this break in our lines and our retirement to the outskirts of Amiens that General Ferdinand Foch was made Allied Commander-in-Chief of all operations. I have been told that during the final stages of our successful though costly retirement, Marshal Foch took Lloyd George, the Prime Minister of Britain, and Clemenceau, the Prime Minister of France, outside the town hall of Doullens and with his walking cane drew a map of the front lines on a large flowerbed and showed these two wonderful leaders how he would beat the Germans. He began by moving large forces of the Americans into the lines in the south to relieve the pressure on the battered French armies, and when the Germans would attack, Foch would order another attack in some other sector of the front. He started moving troops at night and deceiving the enemy as to his intentions. Finally, the enemy was halted around the end of April, 1918, and we began to prepare for an all-out attack which was finally to end in victory on November 11, 1918.

After the wiping out of my old company on March 21st, and shortly after the enemy were held fast before Amiens, I was ordered by division headquarters to report at our base at Etaples for future assignment. This would be around the end of April, 1918. Shortly after my arrival at the base, within a few days at the most, I was given orders to report to another machine gun battalion and first given command of D company of that particular division. The machine gun battalion was under the command of Lieutenant Colonel H.L. Riley, D.S.O., formerly a regular officer of the Rifle Brigade. Colonel Riley was a regular army officer and I say without reservation he was the finest commanding officer I ever served under. Riley understood human nature — he understood men. In this new battalion I was to make friends with an entirely new group of officers, all of whom I grew to regard with great respect. We were now preparing to hit the enemy with everything we could muster. The American army had taken up strong positions in the Ardennes and proven themselves to be a real inspiration to those of us who had seen much more active service. There is no doubt in my mind today that the American nation, whilst it took a long time to realize the danger which was threatening the civilized world, now that they had taken on a specific job, in their usual enthusiastic manner, they threw everything behind their efforts. Without the help of America, it is questionable what would have been the result of the First World War.

Shortly after I took over command of this new company, we relieved one of the other machine gun companies in the front line. We were holding that portion of the front opposite Mount Kemmel, which is located in front of the town of St. Pol, further north of our former positions. The new officers under my command had some experience, most of them having risen from the ranks and been awarded commissions.

The second-in-command of this new company was a Captain J.R. Gooding who was formerly a school teacher and was a very fine officer. I must say that my first experience in the line as commanding officer of this new unit was one of pride — pride not alone that I had risen now to the rank of major, but also because I was proud of the qualities both from a social point of view and a fighting point of view of the fine officers and men under my command. The officers and men were all English. I had grown to admire the fighting qualities of the English soldier, they certainly proved to me beyond any doubt that they were imbued with courage and loyalty. When we of the Colonial regiments take into consideration the fact that these English and Scottish soldiers were being paid a mere one shilling daily, while in some instances the Colonials were receiving five times that amount, the loyalty of our British friends cannot be questioned.

Sometimes I wonder how I rose to a field officer's rank. It may be of interest to relate. When I joined this new machine gun company, our first turn in the line we were attached to a brigade of infantry then under command of a Brigadier James, a regular British officer. James had known Colonel W.H. Franklin, formerly a senior officer in the Newfoundland Regiment, now attached to a British unit, commanding a battalion of infantry. I well remember that first couple of days at Mount Kemmel. The Germans were still trying to drive us back to the Channel ports. We were holding fast. Brigadier General James came around his brigade front, which our machine gun company was protecting. We had learned, as I have related, that never again, after our experience of March 21st, should we place all our guns in forward positions. We made it a rule we should always retain four guns and their crews in reserve. So, in the din of this battle around Mount Kemmel, the General began ticking me off because I had not placed all our guns in the forward positions. He asked me why I had held these four guns in reserve. In fact he was more than severe with me. True to my character, I could not stand it any longer when he continued asking me why I had these guns in reserve and practically ordered me to shift them forward. I refused to do this and told the General I was keeping these guns and their crews in reserve to protect the retreat of brigade headquarters when the old Bosche attacked. He became furious with me and told me that when we came out of the line I would hear from him again. It must have been an act of faith as far as I was concerned, because a couple of days later the Germans attacked our front, piercing it somewhat, and these four guns in reserve came in very useful, as we had to put them into action to protect the flanks of our division and brigade. I felt a bit cocky. I was still wearing the three stars of captain. When we came out to rest, about a week later, the brigadier sent for me. I felt, well, this is IT. He at first told me that we Colonials were too cocky, that we felt we were winning the war all on our own. He ended up by admitting to me that he was wrong and told me he was recommending me for my major's rank, which I received two weeks later.

This new rank was made retroactive to April 1st, and I received additional remuneration and was now wearing the crown insignia on my tunic. I knew that the brigadier could not force me to move these guns. I was the commanding officer of the machine gun company and under our new regulations, the machine gun officer was the individual who laid down the rules and selected the positions where his guns would be placed. The old man found this out later. We became great friends and I always took him around the front line for the remainder of the time we were attached to his brigade.

We were now relieved by a French unit. I found it difficult trying to explain to the French captain who took over from us, the locations of our guns and the necessity of being on the lookout for a German attack. The knowledge I had of the French language was not what one would call proficient, but after an hour or so taking the French officers around the front, we eventually were able to report to our divisional headquarters that we were moving out and that the French were now in position. These French troops were anything but efficient and it was no surprise to me that after a few days of rest as well as pleasure, we were called back to the front to help repel a vicious enemy attack. That French unit appeared to us to be lacking in discipline and leadership.

During the months of May and June, 1918, our armies all along the entire French and Belgian fronts were preparing for a general attack. Under the leadership of Marshal Foch a new spirit had been imbued in all the troops. In addition, the American forces were now actively engaged on the Southern front and had already displayed great courage and bravery. Certainly these American troops were fresh, were becoming accustomed to trench warfare and so were daily making raids and attacks on the enemy lines. Our artillery fire was becoming more and more active, we were being furnished with all kinds of war supplies, both in arms and ammunition. Certainly I must say that the ammunition supplied by the Americans was most deceitful and we were not able to rely on its quality. I had experiences where we would be firing at long range with American ammunition and it would fall short of the target. It became so unreliable that we were forced to dump thousands and thousands of rounds of American ammunition and insist that we be supplied with the

British commodity. The American article was so unreliable that we feared that, in giving indirect fire, we would be shooting our own troops.

During May and June, 1918, our machine gun battalion was continuously in action, both on the offensive and the defensive. We had succeeded, in the month of May, in holding on to our positions and making small advances in some sections. We were in and out of the line continuously. Our entire armies were preparing for an all-out attack. Thousands of guns of all calibres were continuously streaming to the front, guns, which if we had had them six months previously, would have prevented any German advance. Because it was really a matter of luck during the all-out attack by the enemy in March that the entire British Army was not cut off and driven into the English Channel. There is no doubt in many minds, not alone the minds of us junior officers, but the minds of such outstanding men as Lloyd George, Churchill and Clemenceau, that the leadership of our armies was anything but efficient. Thousands upon thousands of lives were sacrificed unnecessarily in order to satisfy the ambitions of our leaders. There is no doubt in the world that under the overall leadership of Foch, who was the outstanding leader of the whole war, that the efforts of all the armies, French, British and American, when co-ordinated under one supreme commander (Foch) were responsible for the turn of the tide in July, 1918. If the Germans made an attack in the south, Foch responded with an attack in the north, whilst the southern allied armies repulsed all efforts of the enemy to make any progress or pierce our lines at any time.

During the last half of June, when we came out for a few days rest, Colonel Riley sent for me and informed me that I was due fourteen days leave of absence. He also told me that I would not be permitted to spend that holiday in Britain, but if I wished I could have ten days leave in Paris, instead. I had never been to Paris, so jumped at the opportunity to visit what is supposed to be the gayest city in the world. I was able to arrange a drive on a motor lorry (French) from our resting village near Doullens down to Amiens. From Amiens, where I had visited frequently before, I took a train into Paris (one or two hours ride). I arrived in Paris one early morning around the end of June, 1918, and went immediately to the Hotel Edward, where I registered, had a good bath and a general clean up before I began looking around.

It had been ten months or thereabouts since I had my last leave and I was fortunate in having the equivalent of about one thousand dollars to my credit in the Bank of Montreal in London. At that time the franc was valued at about 20¢, so I felt well-heeled for my ten days and made up my mind that I was going to see the sights of this wonderful city. Paris was not more than fifty or sixty miles from the trenches as the crow flies, but the people there were carrying on their affairs just as they would in peace time. In fact, it was during my stay there that the first shell from the German Big Bertha fell on Paris. It had been fired from a long range gun built specially for the occasion and it fired that shell from a distance of some sixty odd miles. It did not disturb the equilibrium of the people in any way, and as far as I know it was the only time the gun was used by the enemy. Shortly after, during the Allied advance, the gun was captured, but I never had the pleasure of seeing it.

There were hundreds of officers of the Canadian, American, Australian, New Zealand and British forces on leave at the same time in Paris. I was fortunate in making the acquaintance of a charming New Zealand officer and we did the town together. We visited Napoleon's tomb, the various night clubs and restaurants, not forgetting the famous Folies-Bergères. It is said that one's trip to Paris is never complete without a visit to this famous, or should I say, infamous, music hall. It was a wonderful ten days, continuously on the move, wine, women and song were not overlooked. I met several interesting people, people who were kind and generous and appreciative of our fighting in the cause of France. I can say without hesitation that the ten days I spent in Paris at this time were the gayest in all my life. Wine was cheap and it was an education in itself to sit at a table before some of these cafes on the boulevards, drink wines and liquors to your heart's delight and watch the crowds go by. I believe it is true, what has been said of the Cafe de la Paix, that if one sat at a table before that famous hostelry all day, there is no doubt but one would see someone he knows pass by. I can verify that for myself, because I ran into several officers whom I had trained with at Grantham two years previously. When my ten days leave were finished, I returned to our battalion and my company, tired out and practically broke. It would not be out of order to say that I had to return to active service to get a rest. I had spent July 4th in Paris and, oh, what a day! The American service men on leave from the front and elsewhere were taking over the city. It was not unusual to witness fisticuffs between the Yanks, Frenchmen and British soldiers. The weather was glorious all the time, the heat was intense, and wearing a regulation khaki uniform was anything but pleasant. Fortunately, the evenings were cool and, even though the city was in semi-darkness, life was gay, wine was plentiful and charming women of all calibres were a dime a dozen.

I found my company out of the trenches resting, which was welcome news, as it gave me a little respite, gave me time to catch up on some much-needed rest and sleep. Two days later, having recovered from the effects of a terrifically strenuous holiday, we returned to the trenches and fighting activity, but I could never forget my foolish pleasure and the gaiety and charm of Paris. The place impressed me so much that I made up my mind that any future holidays I had, I would spend in Paris. I had made some very charming friends there. I met English and French families and I remember one very coincidental incident. I had met an English lady and her husband, a Frenchman. They had two sons in the British forces. One was in the Royal Flying Corps and the other was in the British Army. During my time in Paris I had not actually met these two boys, but shortly after I returned to my machine gun company a young officer reported to me for duty. After the usual army ritual, this young officer informed me that he had known of me and referred to his father and mother, whom I had met while in Paris and who had been most kind to me. His name was Harold Gerson. He spoke French just the same as English and had been working on the *Daily Mail* in Paris before the outbreak of war.

Around about the first part of August, 1918, we started to move forward. Our armies had started an offensive against the enemy, making substantial gains. We, therefore, had to move to conform with these advances. At the beginning the going was a bit tough. Each time we were relieved and came back to rest we invariably had further to go when taking up positions after a week or ten days. Our troops were now in great spirits. We were figuring that the war would be over before Christmas and we were wondering what would be our destiny or duties once a surrender came into effect. We were having very few casualties in our unit. Each time we came back off the lines for the usual rest, we took advantage of every spare moment, particularly at night, to celebrate. I remember a lovely little place on the outskirts of Doullens, where we generally went in the evenings for dinner and the usual champagne celebration. Then we would have inter-unit celebrations. All this was most invigorating. Our colonel, whom I have mentioned before, was a great poker player and was always inviting us senior officers to dinner, and after dinner, we would play poker and imbibe whiskey.

Whilst we were making fairly good progress, I do not wish to convey the idea that everything was going really well. We had our difficulties; the Germans did not give up without fighting every inch of the way. Then finally, as October, 1918, was drawing to a close, it was not difficult to see that we were driving the enemy back into his own country. During that forward movement all along the front, with troops of all nationalities, our great problem was to keep our lines of communications open — to keep our forces adequately supplied. We had to forget any kind of comfort, many nights we slept out in the open and under our general service wagons. We had to subsist on what rations we could scrounge and steal. Sometimes, unfortunately, our liquor rations did not arrive on schedule and we cursed and swore at our transport units, knowing full well that they were doing their best, driving their men, horses and mules, as well as any motor transport available. The trenches and grounds all around the front were muddy, yes, muddy is putting it mildly, the weather, at times, was wet and the cold season was fast approaching. We could see that enemy resistance was weakening, his gun fire was getting very intermittent. The old Bosch was dying hard. Around the first of November, we were driving our men and equipment to the limit, but we were joyous and enthusiastic. We could see the end. Then, the night of November 10th came around and the following morning, we received the following order from our headquarters: "HOSTILITIES WILL CEASE AT 11 TODAY ALL LINES WILL BE HELD AND NO INTERCOURSE WILL BE HELD WITH THE ENEMY." We were now holding a line on the main road leading from Mons to Maubeuge, in Belgium. In fact, our troops had occupied Mons and Maubeuge that same morning. To say we were overjoyed would not be overstated. We nearly went mad. We had to stay in that line for several days and then were ordered back and secured very comfortable billets for our officers and men in the Amiens-Doullens area. We were taking life easy. We held the usual army parades daily, but no more drill or training of any sort. We had to clean up all our equipment, etc., and keep that equipment, as well as the guns, in good working condition. As we were close to Amiens, I spent several weekends in Paris and had the usual gay time. I generally took Gerson along with me. He was the interpreter and was useful in getting me through the railway centres. I had discovered that all the railways wanted to permit us on the train from Amiens to Paris was an order from a field officer. My rank as major was a field rank and I made good use of it. During our stay behind the lines we generally had sports of some sort or other a couple of times a week. These were divisional affairs. We had competitions riding horses and mules, running and football competitions, anything to put in time and keep the men in good humor. I must say, our unit was really good and we maintained the usual army discipline. We conducted inspections of the troops every morning and also had inspections of billets.

It was now approaching Christmas, and we made special efforts to see that our men had a most enjoyable time. Some of them were fortunate enough to be permitted to go home for the usual two weeks leave, but had to return at the end of that period. We had no trouble in that respect. Some units had to cancel all leave to England, as many men were taking advantage of the fact that the war was over and there was no necessity of returning. We were also fortunate in that we were not selected to go into Germany. As for me personally, I admit that I would have liked to see Germany in the ordinary course of events, but I had seen enough of Germans and was now concentrating my efforts on getting out of the army as soon as possible. I was still a Newfoundland officer, being merely seconded to the British machine gun corps. How to get out of the British army was now my problem, and it had to be solved. I went to my commanding officer, Colonel Riley, and asked him to take the necessary steps to have me returned to my regiment. After the usual red tape, I was instructed to report to our pay and records office, London, and was told that arrangements were being made to have me return to Newfoundland in the early part of April, 1919. I finally ascertained when the *Digby* would be sailing from Liverpool, and then bid farewell to my officer friends and also the men in "D" company. We had a farewell party at the battalion officers' mess the night before I left our resting billets. In a way I felt sad leaving these fine fellows — I had seen tough times with them during the last six or more months. We had grown to appreciate each other's personalities. All these officers in the four machine gun companies which constituted our machine gun battalion were from English and Scottish regiments and I must say that I worked satisfactorily with them and there was no prejudice or ill-feeling at any time. I had witnessed the last of that old nonsense when we left the machine gun headquarters at Grantham two years previously. There was some difference between Colonel

Riley and Colonel Aplin. Riley was a gentleman —
Aplin was a clown and a snob.

As it would be two or more weeks before the old
Digby was to sail from Liverpool, I decided I would
take a week or so in Paris before going to London and
then to Liverpool. That was some two weeks I can tell
you. I only wish I could describe the details of that
particular ten days. I had made some English and Irish
as well as American friends on my previous visits to the
gay city; and now that I was returning to Newfoundland to be demobilized, they showed me the town in no
uncertain way. There was never a day without excitement and pleasure. I had about one hundred pounds
in money and I certainly did not worry about ex-
penditures until that was finished. Then I left for
London where I spent a few days before embarking on
the *Digby* at Liverpool for Newfoundland.

We had a most enjoyable voyage on the way across
the Atlantic. Among the passengers on the boat were
Mr. William Coaker (later Sir William Coaker) and
Captain John Lewis. They were returning from Italy,
where Captain Lewis had been representing the
Newfoundland government and looking after the interests of the Newfoundland fish exporters. Coaker was
president of the Fishermen's Protective Union and a
member of the then Newfoundland coalition government. I will have much more to say about this man
Coaker in the second volume of this memoir. The
weather was smooth all the way across, not a ripple on
the water. When we came in contact with Cape Race we
were informed by radio that the entire Southern Shore,
Trepassey and St. Mary's Bay, were blocked with ice
and we were forced to go into Placentia Bay, where the
S.S. *Portia,* the coastal steamer, picked us up off
Patrick's Cove and landed us at Argentia. From
Argentia we came into St. John's by special train. Incidentally, passengers on the *Digby* at the same time
were Mr. Harry Hawker and Lieutenant Commander
Mackenzie-Grieve, who were coming to Newfoundland
to attempt a crossing to the United Kingdom by air. The
little airplane in which they were to attempt this
hazardous trip was packed in two large crates and lay

on the fore part of the *Digby*. Hawker was an Australian test pilot during the war, working with the Sopworth Airplane Company, the builders of this little single engine plane. Mackenzie-Grieve was a commander in the British Navy during the war and was to act as Hawker's navigating officer on this proposed trip. They were competing for the five thousand pound prize being donated by the London *Daily Mail* for the first people who would make the direct crossing from Newfoundland to the British Isles. More about this pioneer flying later.

On our arrival that morning in St. John's by train, I was met at the railway station by my father and mother, Sir John Crosbie and several others. I was now in full dress uniform, riding boots and spurs. I had made a special effort the night before to have everything all shined up, the same as if I were going on a general army inspection by a full-blown field marshal. I guess I felt a bit proud of myself at that moment, having left Newfoundland just four years previously as a corporal in the Regiment and returning to Newfoundland as a full-fledged field officer with the rank of major.

The family was now living in Queens Road — Dick had passed away as the result of an accident in November, 1917, Martin, who had been training to fly in the Royal Canadian Air Force, had returned to McGill University to resume his study of medicine, and Larry was a patient in a sanatorium in Ashville, North Carolina, whilst my sister Mary was training to be a nurse in the General Hospital.

I omitted to say that my father had been created a Knight of the British Empire by King George in 1918, and now carried the title, Sir. I was proud of that, as I realized and my readers must realize also, that here was a man who, having begun life in an ordinary fishing boat, had now attained almost the highest position in the country, as well as having attained one of the objects of his great ambition. As we review his active political and commercial life, we see that this man, who started business in 1886 with nothing but ambition and a storehouse of physical and mental energy, which were supported by similar qualities in my mother, had now reached the top of the political, social and commercial ladders. Truly it was a great achievement.

After a few days at home, and after visiting many of my friends, I went to the militia office, was discharged from the Regiment, receiving a bonus of some $150 per month for six months. This was something I did not expect and which came in useful in later months.

Shortly after my return home, the family moved from Queen's Road to King's Bridge Road. Mother later went to North Carolina to bring Larry home, as the doctors there had given him up as a hopeless case of TB, giving him just another six months to live. Forty years later, Larry still alive, had a paralytic stroke and was an invalid for the few remaining years of his life.

This portion of these various incidents in my hectic and stormy life concludes the first twenty-eight years of my existence. In the second volume of this memoir, I will continue my reminiscences, referring to the many sad as well as interesting events of my checkered career. It should then make interesting reading for the younger generation as well as some of those who will survive me, and who may have had some knowledge of events in Newfoundland since the beginning of the twentieth century.